The MAILBOX®

Hooray for Holidays & Seasonal Celebrations® Pre-K

220 Songs, Quick Tips, and Activities

- ☆ New School Year
- ☆ Fall
- ☆ Thanksgiving
- ☆ December Holidays
- ☆ Winter
- ☆ Valentine's Day
- ☆ St. Patrick's Day
- ☆ Spring
- ☆ Parent Days
- ☆ Graduation
- ☆ Summer

Managing Editor: Kelly Robertson

Editorial Team: Becky S. Andrews, Randi Austin, Diane Badden, Kimberley Bruck, Karen A. Brudnak, Marie E. Cecchini, Pam Crane, Kathryn Davenport, Sarah Foreman, Pierce Foster, Deborah Garmon, Deborah Gibbone, Ada Goren, Heather E. Graley, Tazmen Hansen, Marsha Heim, Lori Z. Henry, Lucia Kemp Henry, Roxanne LaBell Dearman, Debra Liverman, Kitty Lowrance, Brenda Miner, Suzanne Moore, Jennifer Nunn, Tina Petersen, Gerri Primak, Mark Rainey, Greg D. Rieves, Hope Rodgers, Leanne Stratton Swinson, Donna K. Teal, Rachael Traylor, Sharon M. Tresino, Virginia Zeletzki

www.themailbox.com

©2009 The Mailbox® Books
All rights reserved.
ISBN10 #1-56234-896-5 • ISBN13 #978-1-56234-896-0

Except as provided for herein, no part of this publication may be reproduced or transmitted in any form or by any means, electronic or mechanical, including photocopying, recording, or storing in any information storage and retrieval system or electronic online bulletin board, without prior written permission from The Education Center, Inc. Permission is given to the original purchaser to reproduce patterns and reproducibles for individual classroom use only and not for resale or distribution. Reproduction for an entire school or school system is prohibited. Please direct written inquiries to The Education Center, Inc., P.O. Box 9753, Greensboro, NC 27429-0753. The Education Center®, *The Mailbox*®, the mailbox/post/grass logo, The Mailbox Book Company® and Holidays & Seasonal Celebrations® are registered trademarks of The Education Center, Inc. All other brand or product names are trademarks or registered trademarks of their respective companies.

What's Inside

Let's Celebrate!

- **96 quick tips**
- **36 songs and rhymes**
- **36 arts-and-crafts activities**
- **52 celebration activities**
- **51 reproducible pages**

Songs and rhymes

Activities

Patterns and practice pages

Look for these symbols!

Songs and More

Arts and Crafts

Time to Celebrate

...and these planning helpers!

Celebration planners

Invitations and Notes

Also programmable online!

Table of Contents

Celebrating a New School Year

Quick Tips

Calendar Time
- Tape a yellow school bus cutout to the end of your classroom pointer.

Centers
- Have students find crayons hidden in a container of colorful paper shreds and sort the crayons by color.
- Place toy school buses at your block center.

Decor
- Display on a bulletin board personal photos and items to help students get to know you.
- Display a large bus cutout. Attach a square photo of each student so he appears to be looking out a bus window.

Good Behavior
- Reward your good apples with apple stickers.

Group Time
- Use colorful crayon cutouts to designate seats in your group area.

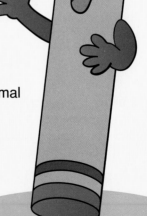

Rest Time
- Encourage each youngster to bring a small stuffed animal from home to be her resting buddy.

Transitions
- As each student gets in line, have him name a classmate to line up behind him.

Songs and More

Welcome, Everyone

Lead youngsters in singing this song to greet their classmates. Repeat the song until each student's name has been used.

(sung to the tune of "Mary Had a Little Lamb")

Welcome, welcome, everyone,
Everyone, everyone!
Welcome, welcome, everyone.
We're glad [child's name]'s at school.

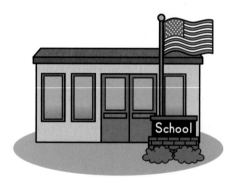

Hooray for School!

Little ones share their excitement about the new school year when they sing this song.

(sung to the tune of "The Farmer in the Dell")

A new school year is here!
A new school year is here!
Oh, hey! Let's say, "Hooray!"
A new school year is here!

Celebrating a New School Year

Tools for School

This catchy tune reminds youngsters of some things they may need at school.

(sung to the tune of "Three Blind Mice")

Crayons, glue,
Scissors too!
In my school bag,
In my school bag,
I've got all the things I need for school.
Just one more thing would make it cool!
A smile on my face is my very best tool
When I'm at school!

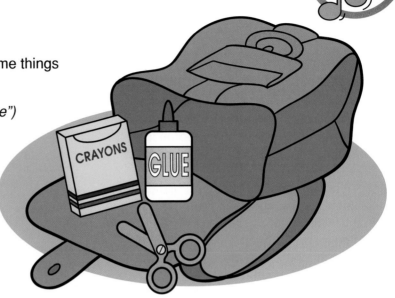

New Friends

Help students learn their classmates' names with this friendly little ditty.

(sung to the tune of "Twinkle, Twinkle, Little Star")

Welcome, welcome, new school friends!
Hope our friendship never ends.
Welcome, [first child's name], and [second child's name] too.
We're so glad to be with you!
Welcome, welcome, new school friends!
Hope our friendship never ends.

Celebrating a New School Year

Arts and Crafts

Personal Placemats

Use these placemats to jazz up the tables at a back-to-school celebration or for snacktime throughout the year. For each student, cut the center from a 12" x 18" sheet of construction paper. A child writes her name on the resulting frame and places it on the sticky side of a piece of clear Con-Tact covering. Then she places inside the frame school-themed die-cut shapes, magazine pictures, and confetti. Help her smooth a second piece of clear Con-Tact covering over the project so the sticky sides meet. Finally, help her trim around the edges of her placemat.

A Beautiful Bouquet

These "hand-some" flowers make a lovely table decoration for a back-to-school celebration. Before beginning the project, place a large ball of play dough in a plastic flowerpot or other decorative container. A student lightly sets his hand in paint and then makes a handprint on white paper. When the paint is dry, help him write his name on the palm and then cut around the handprint. Tape a straw to the back of each print and place the resulting flowers in the pot.

Celebrating a New School Year • • • • • • • • • •

Great Work Magnet

These simple magnetic clips allow parents to proudly display their youngsters' work. To make one, help a child personalize a tagboard copy of a crayon box pattern from page 15. Then she uses various craft supplies to decorate her crayon box. She cuts out the box and glues it to a wooden clothespin. After the glue is dry, attach a strip of magnetic tape to the clothespin.

Tools I Use

To make a mobile, a child uses various craft materials to decorate a backpack (pattern on page 16); then he cuts the backpack out. He colors and cuts apart a copy of the school supply cards from page 17. Next, he tapes one end of a length of yarn to the back of each card and the other end to the back of the backpack. Finally, help him punch a hole near the top of the backpack and add a yarn loop for hanging.

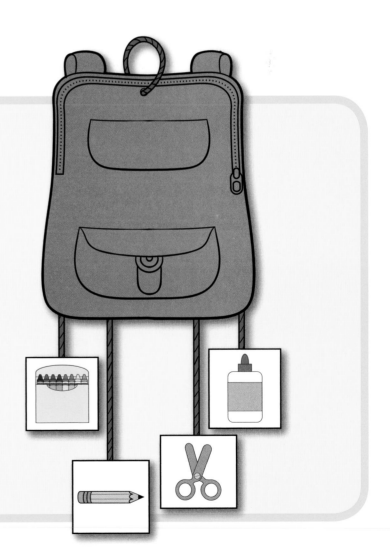

Celebrating a New School Year

Time to Celebrate!

First Day Fun

Send these booklets home so youngsters can tell their families about their first day of school. Help each child personalize a copy of page 18. Instruct her to cut out the booklet backing and pages and then order the pages atop the backing. Staple the booklet for her and have her draw herself on the cover. Then read aloud each text page and have her illustrate the page.

Then and Now

After completing this activity, tuck students' projects away until the end of the school year. Give each student a 12" x 18" sheet of white construction paper folded in half. Instruct him to open the paper and draw a self-portrait on the left side of the paper. Label the drawing with his name and the date. File the finished papers for safekeeping. At the end of the school year, give each student his paper folded so that his drawing is facedown and the blank side is up. Have him draw another self-portrait and help him write his name and the date. Encourage each child to unfold his paper and compare his drawings to see the progress he's made.

Jason
August 25, 2009

Jason
May 27, 2010

Celebrating a New School Year

My New Class

Help students get to know their classmates with this class book. For each child, attach her photo to a sheet of paper. Help her write her name below the photo; then invite her to decorate her paper. Collect students' finished pages and bind them to make a book. At group time, read the book aloud. Once students are familiar with their classmates' names, cover the name on each page and encourage volunteers to name the pictured student.

Make a Wish

This activity encourages students to think about things they want to do during the school year. To begin, assist students in brainstorming a wish list of things they want to do at school. Invite each child to choose a wish from the list as you write it on a slip of paper along with his name. Then have youngsters put their slips in a wish jar (a clean plastic jar decorated as desired). Set the wish jar aside. At the end of the school year, return each wish to the child who made it. Invite him to share his wish with the class and announce whether it came true.

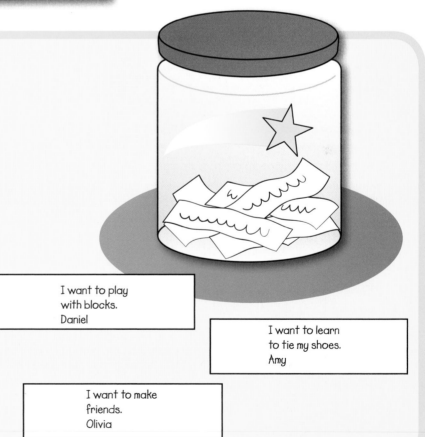

I want to play
with blocks.
Daniel

I want to learn
to tie my shoes.
Amy

I want to make
friends.
Olivia

Celebrating a New School Year

Backpack Memory

Test students' visual memory with this simple game. Display a child's backpack and a few basic school supplies, such as a pair of scissors, a box of crayons, a pencil, a glue stick, and a pencil box. Invite students to study the supplies for a few moments; then ask them to cover their eyes. Hide one or two supplies in the backpack. Have students uncover their eyes and ask volunteers to name the missing items. For an added challenge, hide all the supplies in the backpack; then, as students name each supply, remove it.

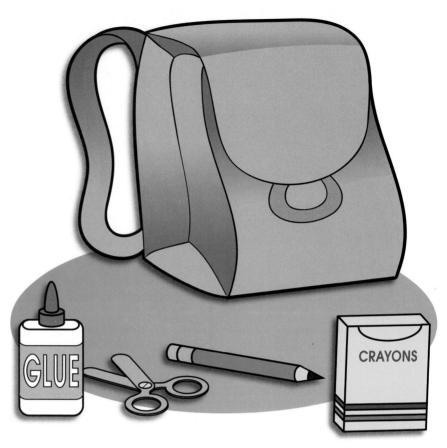

Tasty School Bus

Ingredients for one:
whole graham cracker
yellow-tinted frosting
square cereal pieces (windows)
2 mini chocolate sandwich cookies (wheels)

Preparation: Break apart the sections of the graham cracker and then break one section in half. Discard one half of the broken section.

Directions: To make a bus shape, have each child place the graham cracker pieces as shown. Then invite her to spread frosting on the crackers. Direct her to add windows and wheels to complete the bus.

Celebrating a New School Year

Celebration Planner

To do:

Planned activities:

Reminders:

Volunteer	Contact Number	Email

We Are Celebrating!

Please join us at _____ on
time

_____, _____,
day date

as we celebrate _____

_____

_____

_____.

We hope to see you!

Hooray for Holidays & Seasonal Celebrations® • ©The Mailbox® Books • TEC61236

_____'s

First day of school was great!

_____   _____
teacher date

Hooray for Holidays & Seasonal Celebrations® • ©The Mailbox® Books • TEC61236

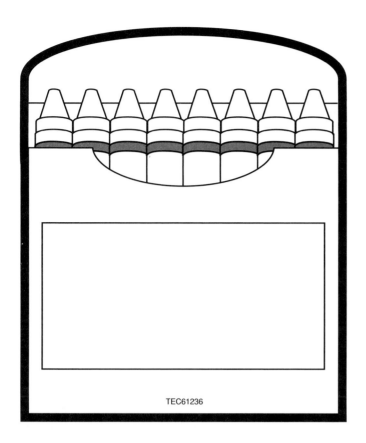

TEC61236

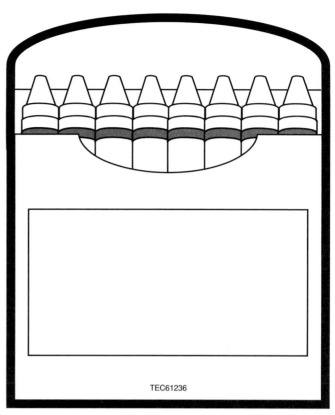

TEC61236

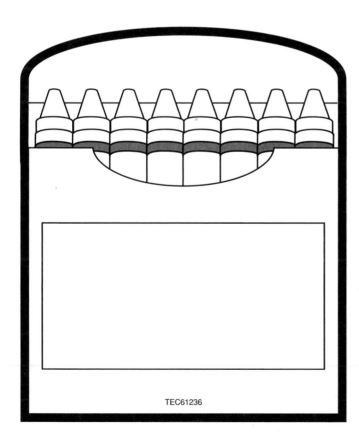

TEC61236

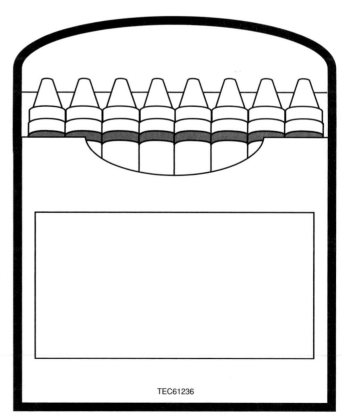

TEC61236

Backpack Pattern
Use with "Tools I Use" on page 9.

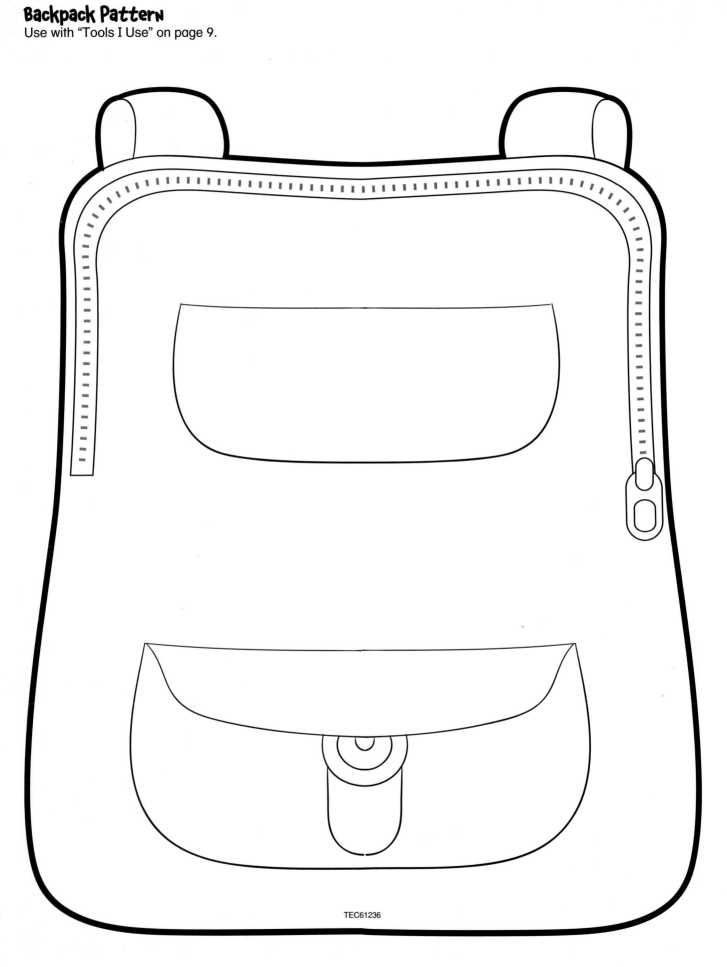

TEC61236

 Hooray for Holidays & Seasonal Celebrations® • ©The Mailbox® Books • TEC61236

TEC61236

TEC61236

TEC61236

TEC61236

Booklet Backing and Pages

Use with "First Day Fun" on page 10.

1

_____'s

First Day

Hooray for Holidays & Seasonal Celebrations® • ©The Mailbox® Books • TEC61236

3

a new friend

4

School

a fun activity

2

my teacher

Celebrating Fall

Quick Tips

Calendar Time

- Attach an acorn cutout to your classroom pointer.
- Discuss the fall months and the special events and holidays that occur during them.

Centers

- Fill your sand table with crunchy leaves.
- Place magnifying glasses at your sensory center along with a variety of fall items, such as mini pumpkins and gourds, leaves, and Indian corn.

Decor

- Attach student-created fall leaves to a tree display. Mount little ones' artwork on the display with the title "Falling for Amazing Art!"

Good Behavior

- Pull a leaf cutout from a tree display and attach it at the base of the tree each time good behavior is observed. When all the leaves have been relocated, provide a reward to the class.

Group Time

- Display a large tub of water and a small pumpkin. Ask students whether they think the pumpkin will float when it is placed in the water. Label the columns of a two-column chart "yes" and "no" and invite each youngster to attach a personalized sticky note in the column matching her prediction. Then place the pumpkin in the water and lead little ones in discussing the result.

Rest Time

- Invite students to float and twirl to their rest mats as if they were falling leaves.

Songs and More

Autumn Is Here

Little ones are sure to enjoy this musical welcome to fall.

(sung to the tune of "The Itsy-Bitsy Spider")

Autumn is here right now.
The leaves are falling down.
They float from the trees.
They're yellow, red, and brown.
We see orange pumpkins glowing in the sun.
When the season is fall, it is fun for everyone!

Big Orange Pumpkins

Incorporate fall props—such as seed cutouts, green yarn, a tissue paper flower, a pumpkin, and a jack-o'-lantern—to make this pumpkin tune come to life.

(sung to the tune of "My Bonnie Lies Over the Ocean")

I planted a seed in my garden.
It sprouted and grew into a vine.
Then soon there were blossoms so orange
That grew into pumpkins so fine.

Big, orange pumpkins,
They grow on a vine on the ground, you see.
Then I'll carve them
And make jack-o'-lanterns for me!

Spooky Jack-o'-Lanterns

Add motions to this jolly tune and create an entertaining performance for family and friends.

(sung to the tune of "Do Your Ears Hang Low?")

Plant some pumpkin seeds
In your little garden row.
Give them lots of water.
Then watch them start to grow.

When they're big and orange,
We'll make jack-o'-lanterns too.
And we'll all say, "Boo!"

Bend down as if planting seeds.

Water with pretend watering can.
*Place hand above eyebrows and look
 back and forth.*
Make a big circle with arms.

*Put hands over eyes and open hands
 on "Boo!"*

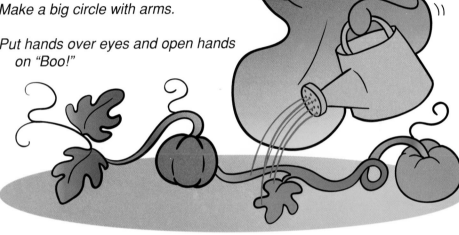

Halloween Fun

Little folks and big folks will enjoy this happy Halloween tune!

(sung to the tune of "Down by the Station")

Halloween is spooky.
It comes just once a year.
There are bats and spiders
When Halloween is near.
We see ghosts and goblins,
But you must never fear
'Cause when Halloween is over
They will disappear!

Celebrating Fall

Arts and Crafts

Halloween Headbands

Here's a fun way for little ones to dress up for a class-room celebration without all the costume commotion! Attach a seasonal cutout to a tagboard strip for each child. Invite the student to decorate his strip and add embellishments to the cutout. Then staple the strip to fit his head. He can proudly wear his headband during the party!

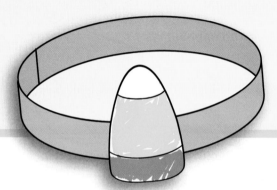

Pumpkin Patch Prints

To create this delightful display, paint the palm of each youngster's hand with orange paint and press it on paper to make a pumpkin. Next, have her dip her thumb in green paint to make a stem at the top. When the paint is dry, have her cut out the pumpkin. Make vines by twisting brown craft paper into a rope shape and painting it green. To make a backdrop for an autumn festival, attach the vines to a bulletin board in rows and add leaves and the palm print pumpkins.

Seasonal Stampers

Invite little ones to design their own autumn placemats to use during a classroom party. To make a stamper, cut a potato in half. Press a fall-shaped cookie cutter into the cut side of one potato half. Use a knife to cut away the excess potato from around the cutter and then remove the cutter from the potato. After creating several different stampers, guide each child to dip the potatoes in paint and make prints on a large sheet of construction paper. If desired, laminate the finished placemats for durability.

Spooky Lanterns

This craft can be hung from the ceiling or placed on the tables to brighten any Halloween celebration! To make a spider lantern, paint four fingers and the palm of a child's hand with black paint. Assist him in making prints of his hand in several different places on a 12" x 18" sheet of orange construction paper (bordered with black paper, if desired). Then turn the child's hand so the fingers face the opposite direction and make additional prints, overlapping the palm portion of each of the original prints. Once the paint has dried, add hole reinforcer eyes to each spider, roll the paper into a cylinder, and staple it in place. Punch two holes at the top of the cylinder and thread yarn through the holes to hang the lantern.

Celebrating Fall

Time to Celebrate!

Easy as Pie!

Ingredients for one:
graham cracker crumbs
apple or pumpkin pie filling
whipped cream

Directions: Help a child put two spoonfuls of graham cracker crumbs in a cup. Have her add three spoonfuls of pie filling. Then invite her to top the pie filling with one spoonful of whipped cream before she enjoys her autumn treat!

Gathering Nuts

This whole-group game will send your little squirrels scampering on a fun nut hunt! To prepare, hide acorn cutouts around the room. As you recite the rhyme below, direct youngsters to search for the hidden cutouts and return to the group with acorns in hand.

Little squirrels, little squirrels,
Gather nuts you see.
Look up high
And look down low.
Then scamper back to me!

Celebrating Fall

"Whoooo's" Ready for Fall?

This table decoration will be a hoot at home or in the classroom! To make an owl centerpiece, copy and cut out for each child a set of the owl patterns (page 28) on yellow, brown, and white construction paper as directed. Assist each little one in gluing the eyes, wings, beak, and head feathers on a brown paper lunch bag as shown. Invite him to add additional details with crayons or markers. When the glue has dried, he stuffs the bag with newspaper shreds and closes it with a rubber band. Have him place his owl on a piece of cardboard tube so it is self-standing.

Pass the Candy

There will be no tricks—only treats—when students gather to play this Halloween game! To prepare, program a class supply of candy cards (page 29) with shapes, letters, or numbers; then cut apart the cards and place them in a trick-or-treat container. To begin, pass the container around the circle as you play a recording of spooky music. When you stop the music, the child holding the container pulls a card, identifies what is written on the candy, and places the card in front of her. Continue play until all the cards have been removed from the container.

Find a reproducible activity on page 30!

Celebrating Fall

Celebration Planner

To do:

Planned activities:

Reminders:

Volunteer	Contact Number	Email

Hooray for Holidays & Seasonal Celebrations • ©The Mailbox® Books • TEC61236

Fantastic Fall Festival!

Please join us at _____ on
time

_____, _____,
day   date

as we celebrate _____

_____

_____

_____.

We hope to see you!

Hooray for Holidays & Seasonal Celebrations® • ©The Mailbox® Books • TEC61236

Autumn Reminders

Hooray for Holidays & Seasonal Celebrations® • ©The Mailbox® Books • TEC61236

Owl Patterns
Use with " 'Whoooo's' Ready for Fall?" on page 25.

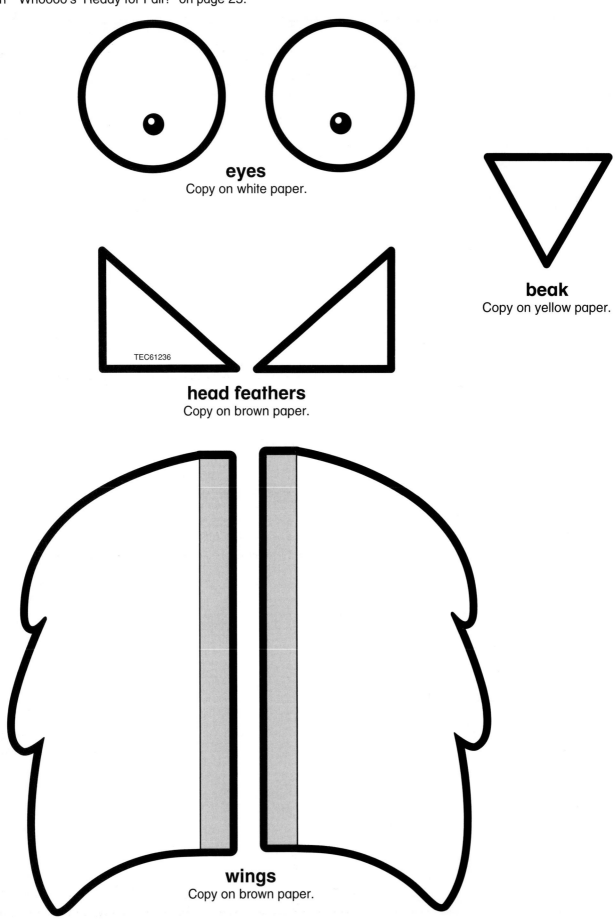

eyes
Copy on white paper.

beak
Copy on yellow paper.

TEC61236

head feathers
Copy on brown paper.

wings
Copy on brown paper.

Hooray for Holidays & Seasonal Celebrations® • ©The Mailbox® Books • TEC61236

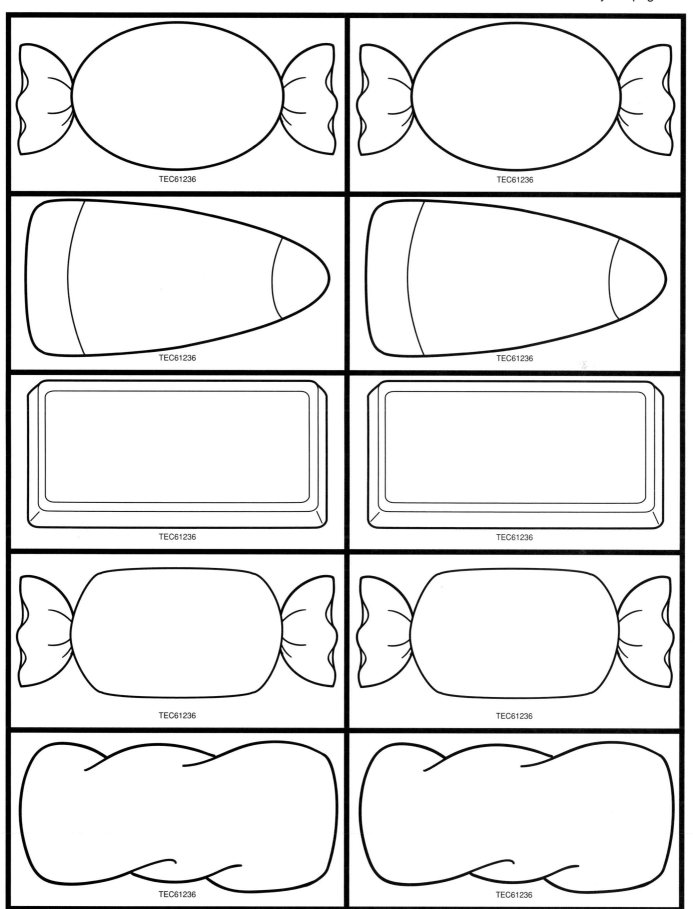

TEC61236

TEC61236

TEC61236

TEC61236

TEC61236

TEC61236

TEC61236

TEC61236

TEC61236

TEC61236

Acorn Hunt

Trace.
Color.

Celebrating Thanksgiving

Quick Tips

Calendar Time

- Include a thankful thought each day.
- Tape colorful craft feathers to the end of your classroom pointer.

Centers

- Put a few gourds at your sensory center.
- Fill your sand table with corn feed.

Cleanup

- Invite little ones to waddle and gobble like turkeys during cleanup time.

Dismissal

- Substitute "gobble, gobble!" for "goodbye!"

Good Behavior

- Remind students how thankful you are for their good behavior.
- Attach class-earned stickers to a classroom Plymouth Rock—a large rock-shaped paper cutout.

Group Time

- Outline your group area with a trail of turkey tracks made from masking tape, or mark individual places with tracks.

Songs and More

Feeling Thankful

Lead little ones and guests in this crowd-pleasing version of a familiar song.

(sung to the tune of "If You're Happy and You Know It")

If you're thankful and you know it, clap your hands. *(Clap, clap.)*
If you're thankful and you know it, clap your hands. *(Clap, clap.)*
If you're thankful and you know it,
You can't be afraid to show it.
If you're thankful and you know it, clap your hands. *(Clap, clap.)*

Additional verses:
If you're thankful and you know it, say you are. *(I am!)*
If you're thankful and you know it, give a wave. *(Wave, wave.)*
If you're thankful and you know it, do all three. *(Clap, clap. I am!
Wave, wave.)*

Thanksgiving Togetherness

After singing this song, encourage students and guests to share their favorite Thanksgiving tradition.

(sung to the tune of "My Bonnie Lies Over the Ocean")

Thanksgiving's a special time of year
When we show people that we care.
We gather together with family.
Thanksgiving's a great time to share!

Thanksgiving Feast

Incorporate dramatic-play props, and this fun-to-sing song becomes a musical production.

(sung to the tune of "Clementine")

Mashed potatoes, sweet potatoes,
Some green beans, and berry pie.
Give me turkey; give me stuffing.
Put my gravy on the side.

I'm so happy. I'm so thankful.
I'm so full I might just pop.
But it doesn't seem to matter
'Cause I sure can't seem to stop!

Turkey Superstars

This turkey activity is especially fun when performed onstage! Have students act out the rhyme as you read it aloud.

[Number of students] turkeys standing in a row,   *Stand in a row.*
They spread their wings and tails just so.   *Stretch arms out to sides and wiggle hips.*
They gobble to the left;   *Gobble and look left.*
Next, they gobble to the right.   *Gobble and look right.*
Then they strut their stuff. It's really quite a sight!   *Strut enthusiastically.*
But don't ask to see the turkeys on Thanksgiving Day   *Act alarmed.*
For not a single one will come out to play!   *Hurry offstage.*

Arts and Crafts

Gobbling Good Placemats

Help each child trace one of his hands on the center of a 12" x 18" sheet of tan construction paper (placemat). Then he colors the tracing and draws details so it looks like a turkey. Write on his placemat the words "Gobble, gobble!" the child's name, and the current year; then laminate it for durability. Invite students to use the placemats at your Thanksgiving party and also for their Thanksgiving meals at home.

Gobble, gobble!

Jack

2009

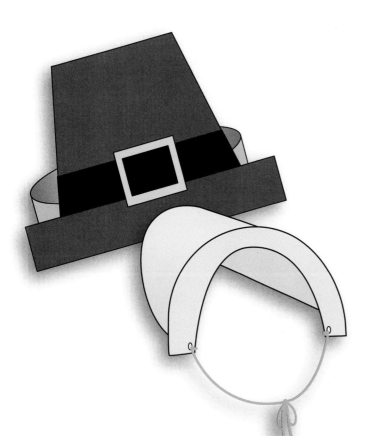

Party Hats

With these timely hat options, there's no need to fret over costumes.

Pilgrim Hat: Make the hat from construction paper and then tape the project to a tagboard headband.

Pilgrim Bonnet: Hole-punch a tagboard strip, as shown, and tie a length of yarn to the ends; then staple the straight edge of a semicircle cutout to the strip.

Celebrating Thanksgiving

Colorful Cornucopias

In advance, use white glue to make crisscross lines on a sheet of tagboard. After the glue is dry, a child places a sheet of white paper over the glue lines and rubs the side of an unwrapped brown crayon over the paper. Next, he traces a tagboard cornucopia on the paper, cuts the tracing out, and glues the cutout to a sheet of paper. Then he dips fruit- and vegetable-shaped sponges in shallow containers of paint to make prints on his project.

A Classy Turkey

The result of this project is a well-dressed turkey! Display an enlarged copy of the featherless turkey pattern from page 41. Then cut out a supply of turkey feathers sized to fit the turkey. Provide little ones with a variety of craft supplies and invite them to decorate their feathers as desired. Help each child add her completed feather to the turkey.

Celebrating Thanksgiving

Time to Celebrate!

Active Turkeys

This whole-group game combines gross-motor and listening skills. To begin, have students stand in an open area with plenty of space between them. Announce a movement such as "Turkeys, jump!" Students perform the movement until you say, "Turkeys, stop!" Consider having your little turkeys perform movements such as hopping on one foot, spinning, running in place, or stretching.

Turkeys, clap!

Miguel

Mini Mayflowers

These small ships can double as place cards at your Thanksgiving celebration. For each child, cut one side off a clean individual-size milk carton. To make a ship, a student paints the outside of his carton with a mixture of brown tempera paint and white glue. (It may be necessary to apply two coats of paint to cover the print on the carton.) After the paint is dry, he writes his name on a white paper rectangle (sail) and then tapes it and another sail to a wooden stir stick. Next, the child places a small ball of clay inside his carton and stands the stick in the clay.

Celebrating Thanksgiving

A Thankful Wreath

Have each child draw on a fall-colored leaf cutout a picture of something for which she is thankful. Invite each child to share her picture with the group. Then help youngsters glue their leaves to a tagboard circle to make a wreath. After each child's leaf is attached to the wreath, write "We Are Thankful" in the wreath's center. Display the completed wreath during your celebration as a reminder of the things for which students are thankful.

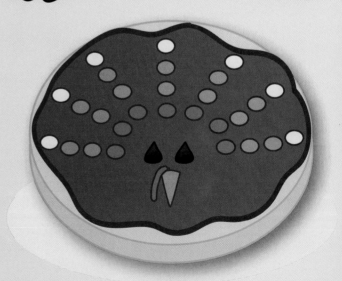

A Perky Turkey

Ingredients for one:
round sugar cookie
dollop of chocolate frosting
M&M's Minis candy
2 mini chocolate chips
small triangle of an orange fruit-flavored snack
small strip of a red fruit-flavored snack

Directions: Have each child spread frosting on her cookie and place the M&M's candy along the cookie's top half, as shown, so the candy looks like feathers. Then have her use the chocolate chips and fruit snack pieces to make a turkey face on the cookie. Finally, invite her to gobble up her tasty treat!

Celebrating Thanksgiving

Turkey Egg?

Your students will be all "a-gobble" over this group game. To make a turkey egg (a creamy-tan egg with brown speckles), tightly wad newspaper into an oversize egg shape. Wrap the newspaper in masking tape and use a brown marker to add speckles. To begin play, choose two children to wait outside the classroom while another child hides the turkey egg inside. Once the egg is hidden, the waiting students return and are given single-word clues about the egg's location. Examples might include "sink" and "under," or "teacher" and "desk" and "beside." The two students discuss the clues and then tell their guess. If the guess is correct, the class gobbles.

Thankful Thoughts

This quiet-time booklet project serves as a reminder of the meaning of Thanksgiving! In advance, make a class supply of the booklet cover and pages on pages 42 and 43. Use a paper cutter to cut apart the covers and pages; then assemble a booklet for each child, stapling along each booklet's left margin. First, have each student write her name on the cover and color the artwork. Next, read aloud the first booklet page and ask her to draw and color a picture of the home for which she is thankful. Proceed in a like manner until all booklet pages are illustrated. Send the heartwarming projects home for youngsters to share with their families.

Find a reproducible activity on page 44!

Celebrating Thanksgiving

Celebration Planner

To do:

Planned activities:

Reminders:

Volunteer	Contact Number	Email

We Are Celebrating!

Please join us at _____ on

time

_____ , _____ ,

day   date

as we celebrate _____

_____

_____

_____.

We hope to see you!

Hooray for Holidays & Seasonal Celebrations® • ©The Mailbox® Books • TEC61236

Date _____

Gobbling Good News!

Hooray for Holidays & Seasonal Celebrations® • ©The Mailbox® Books • TEC61236

TEC61236

I Am Thankful

by _____

Hooray for Holidays & Seasonal Celebrations® • ©The Mailbox® Books • TEC61236

I am thankful for my home so sweet.

①

I am thankful for the food I eat.

②

I am thankful for the things I have and do.

③

I am thankful for my friends, old and new.

④

I am thankful for my family too!

⑤

Happy Thanksgiving!

Color.

Cut.

Glue.

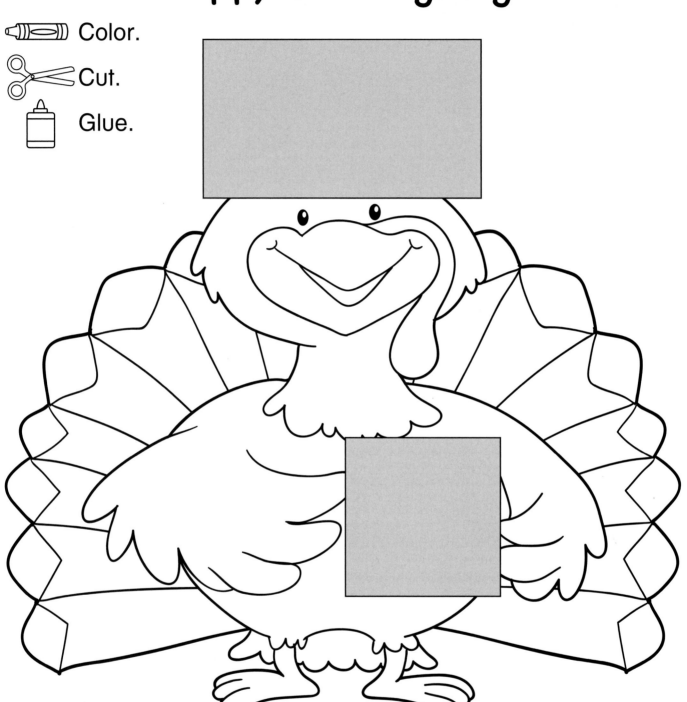

Hooray for Holidays & Seasonal Celebrations® • ©The Mailbox® Books • TEC61236

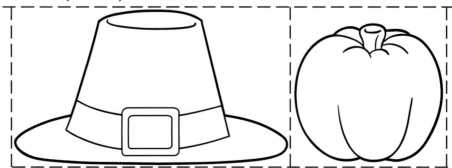

Celebrating December Holidays

Quick Tips

Calendar Time

- Use a candy cane as your classroom pointer.
- Attach holiday-related shapes to important dates; then count down to the corresponding holidays and special events.

Centers

- Place gift bows at your math center for counting, sorting, and patterning.
- Add holiday gift-wrapping supplies to your dramatic-play center.

Cleanup

- Shake holiday bells to signal cleanup time.

Good Behavior

- Attach festive stickers to a holiday cutout—such as a unity cup, a dreidel, or a stocking—when the class exhibits exceptionally good behavior.

Group Time

- Display several holiday-related items; then cover them with a festive cloth. Secretly remove an item and whisk the cloth away. Invite students to guess what is missing.

Rest Time

- Play a recording of soothing holiday music.

Transitions

- Play holiday music and have little ones pass around a gift box while they wait to wash their hands. When the music stops, the child holding the gift box takes his turn washing his hands.
- Provide clues to help youngsters identify a predetermined holiday item.

Songs and More

Christmastime

Invite youngsters to spread holiday cheer by singing this fun song.

(sung to the tune of "Twinkle, Twinkle, Little Star")

Christmastime is almost here.
Christmas comes just once a year.
We help decorate the tree.
It's a time for family.
We will get some gifts and toys
For being good girls and boys!

My Kinara

Sing this nifty tune during a holiday celebration! To add to the fun, provide three red candles, three green candles, and one black candle for volunteers to hold in the air at the appropriate time.

(sung to the tune of "If You're Happy and You Know It")

In my kinara, seven candles burning bright!
In my kinara, they will shine for seven nights.
They are red and black and green,
Prettiest lights you've ever seen!
In my kinara, seven candles burning bright!

Celebrating December Holidays

Festival of Lights

Light up your Hanukkah celebration with this lively ditty!

(sung to the tune of "Yankee Doodle")

On Hanukkah we celebrate.
It's the Festival of Lights.
We light the candles, and they glow
On each of eight dark nights.
We can open up our gifts
And eat latkes too.
Hanukkah's a special time
With lots of things to do!

Happy New Year!

Have youngsters use musical instruments or noisemakers to ring in the new year following the chant at the end of this song!

(sung to the tune of "Shoo Fly")

Goodbye! This year is done!
Tonight we'll have some fun.
Midnight is almost here.
Then we'll start a brand new year!

Chant:
Ten! Nine! Eight! Seven! Six!
Five! Four! Three! Two! One!
Happy New Year!

Celebrating December Holidays

Arts and Crafts

Starry Napkin Rings

These festive napkin rings will make any party table sparkle. To make a Christmas napkin ring, a child paints a section of cardboard tube yellow and then sets it aside to dry. Next, she spreads a mixture of gold glitter and glue on a yellow star cutout. When the mixture is dry, she glues the star to the tube. To make a Hanukkah napkin ring, she uses blue paint, a mixture of silver glitter and glue, and a blue six-point star cutout.

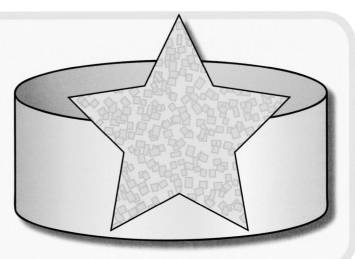

Musical Shakers

Decorative shakers add musical entertainment to your holiday celebrations. A child paints the backs of two small paper plates a holiday color. When the paint is dry, he adds decorations, such as holiday cutouts or stickers. When he is finished decorating, staple the rims of the plates together, leaving a small opening. Finally, pour rice through the opening and staple it closed.

Reindeer Place Cards

Using place cards at a celebration makes seating simple and adds to the holiday decor. To make one, a child folds a blank 4" x 6" card in half as shown. She dips a circular sponge in brown paint and then presses it onto the folded index card to make the reindeer's head. When the paint is dry, she draws antlers and eyes with a thin black marker. Then she glues on a red mini pom-pom for a nose. To complete the project, she writes her name on the place card, with help as needed.

Delightful Dreidels

Showcase these sun-catching dreidels as part of your Hanukkah decorations! To make one, a child presses a blue construction paper dreidel-shaped frame to the sticky side of a piece of Con-Tact covering. Next, he presses yellow and blue tissue paper squares within the frame. Cover the dreidel with another sheet of Con-Tact covering and trim any excess. Mount the projects in a window or suspend them from the ceiling to watch them spin!

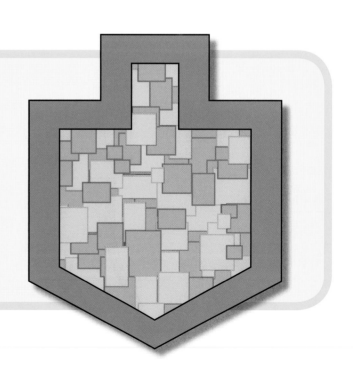

Celebrating December Holidays

Time to Celebrate!

Spin, Spin, Spin!

For this whole-group game, a student (dreidel) secretly chooses an item in the classroom. Then she slowly spins around as you lead the remaining youngsters in chanting, "Spinning dreidel, spinning dreidel, what do you see?" At the end of the chant, the dreidel stops spinning and gives a clue to help identify the item. A volunteer tries to guess the item. If his guess is correct, he becomes the dreidel. If it is incorrect, the dreidel spins around again and provides another clue. If the item is not identified after several clues, the dreidel reveals the object and chooses a classmate to be the new dreidel.

In My Stocking

Youngsters will be eager to share their holiday wishes in this adorable booklet! In advance, make a copy of pages 56 and 57 for each child. Also cut out two red construction paper stockings for each child (booklet covers) and program the cover as shown. Have each child personalize her cover. Next, read aloud the text on page one of the booklet; then have each child illustrate the page. Continue in the same way with the remaining pages. Finally, help each child cut out her pages, stack them in order between the booklet covers, and then staple along the top. If desired, have her glue cotton batting to the front cover as shown.

Celebrating December Holidays

Keepsake Card

This handmade card is sure to be a cherished memento. Give each child a copy of page 55 and have her draw a picture of herself with the intended recipient inside the picture frame. Next, have her write or dictate a special message on the card. Help her write her name on the line and then cut out the card. To complete this holiday keepsake, help her fold the card along the center line. Finally, have her decorate the front of the card.

Stocking Stuffer Relay

In advance, gather an even number of Christmas stockings that will easily slide onto youngster's feet. Have each child remove his shoes; then divide the class into teams and have them sit on the floor. Give one child on each team a pair of stockings. Shake holiday bells to start the game. Each student slides the stockings on and then off his feet as quickly as he can; then he passes the pair of stockings to the next child. As teams finish, they cheer on their classmates until every team is done.

Celebrating December Holidays

Candy Cane Cookies

Ingredients for one:
miniature candy cane (in a resealable
    plastic bag)
sugar cookie
white frosting

Preparation: Have each child use a
wooden block to crush a candy cane into
small pieces; then set the bag aside.

Directions: Have each youngster spread
a dollop of frosting on a cookie; then have
her sprinkle the crushed candy cane on
the frosting. Invite her to taste this sweet
peppermint treat!

Reindeer Muffins

Ingredients for one:
English muffin half
2 chocolate chips
maraschino cherry
6 pretzel sticks
whipped cream cheese (tinted brown)

Preparation: Toast the muffin halves.

Directions: Have each child spread a
dollop of cream cheese on his muffin half.
Then instruct him to lightly press the chocolate chips (eyes) and the cherry (nose) into
the cream cheese. To complete the reindeer, help him push pretzel sticks (antlers)
into the top of the muffin.

Find a
reproducible activity
on page 58!

Celebrating December Holidays

Celebration Planner

To do:

Planned activities:

Reminders:

Volunteer	Contact Number	Email

We Are Celebrating!

Please join us at _____ on
                      time

_____, _____,
        day   date

as we celebrate

_____

_____

_____.

We hope to see you!

Hooray for Holidays & Seasonal Celebrations® • ©The Mailbox® Books • TEC61236

Help Make Our Holiday Celebration a Success!

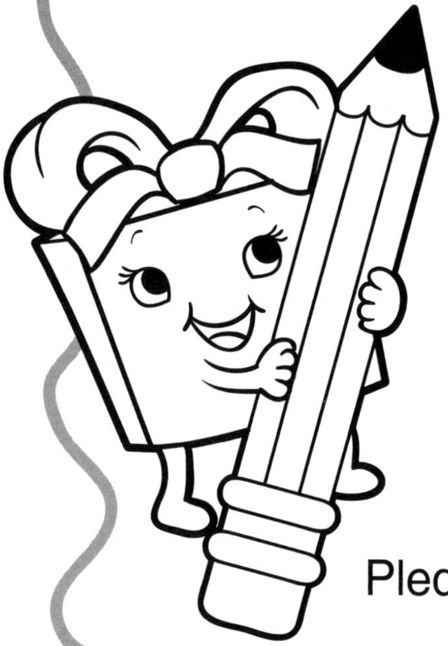

Items Needed

_____   _____

_____   _____

_____   _____

_____   _____

_____   _____

Please contact _____
                          name

at _____ before _____.
   phone number/email address   date

Hooray for Holidays & Seasonal Celebrations® • ©The Mailbox® Books • TEC61236

Handmade With Love!

From _____

1

TEC61236

Something to wear.

Something to eat.

2

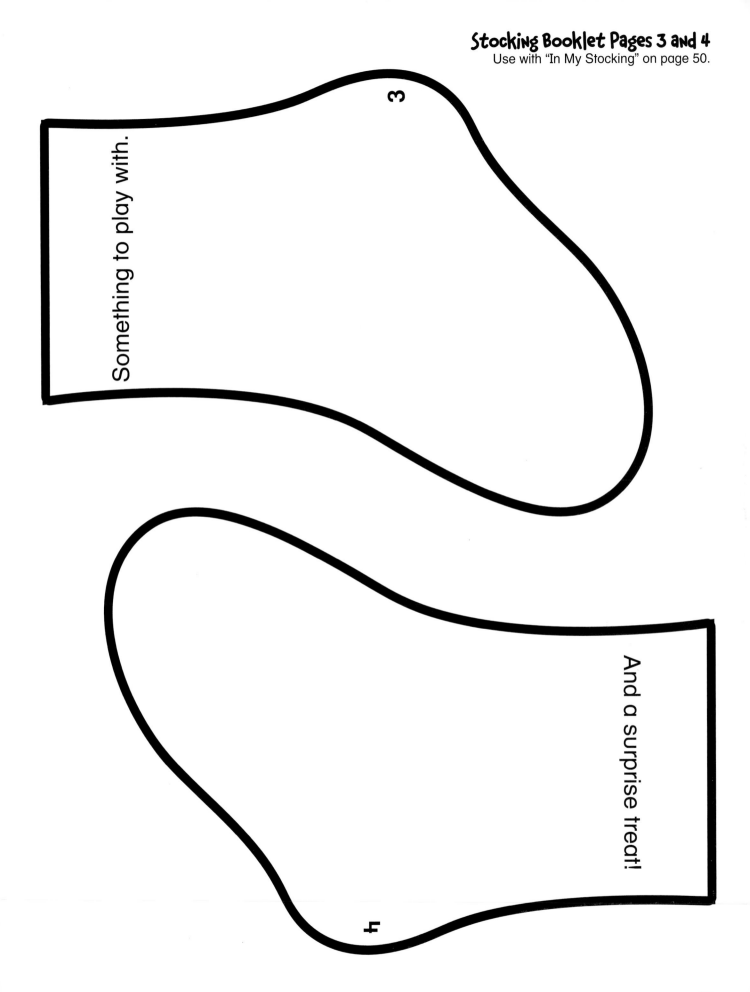

Something to play with.

3

And a surprise treat!

4

Pretty Present

Connect the dots in order from 1 to 20.

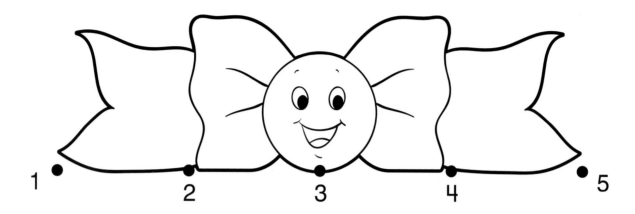

1

20

19

18

17

16

15

2

3

4

14

13

12

5

6

7

8

9

10

11

Hooray for Holidays & Seasonal Celebrations® • ©The Mailbox® Books • TEC61236

Note to the teacher: After a student connects the dots, have her cut or tear gift wrap scraps and glue them to the paper to decorate the gift.

Celebrating Winter

Quick Tips

Calendar Time

- Tape a snowpal cutout to your classroom pointer.
- Attach a snowflake sticker to the calendar each day it snows.

Centers

- Set out hole punchers, scissors, and white paper and invite youngsters to make paper snow.
- Freeze water in a baking pan. Invite little ones to manipulate plastic people and animals to "skate" on the ice.

Cleanup

- Encourage students to wear their mittens or scarves during cleanup time.

Good Behavior

- Have the Snow Fairy leave a snowflake cutout on the seat of each student who exhibits good behavior.
- Each time the class demonstrates good behavior, add a mini marshmallow to a plastic mug. When the mug is full, treat youngsters to a special snack or privilege.

Group Time

- Roll a white foam ball (snowball) to a student to indicate her turn to speak.
- Place mounds of cotton batting (snow) on the floor to designate students' seats.

Rest Time

- At the end of rest time, encourage little ones to pretend they are bears waking at the beginning of spring.

Songs and More

Fun in the Snow

Little ones will be eager to play in the snow after singing this little ditty!

(sung to the tune of "Twinkle, Twinkle, Little Star")

Snow is falling all around.
Fluffy snow is on the ground.
Let's catch snowflakes on our tongues.
Then build snowmen—oh, what fun!
Snow is falling all around.
Fluffy snow is on the ground.

Winter Wear

Sing this song to remind youngsters about the clothing they should wear in the snow.

(sung to the tune of "Where Is Thumbkin?")

Grab your mittens,
Grab your mittens
And your coat,
And your coat.
Don't forget your snow boots,
Your scarf, and your warm hat.
Let's go play
In the snow!

Snowy Day

Invite students to add simple actions to this song to create a musical performance.

(sung to the tune of "Up on the Housetop")

It started snowing—where's my coat?
Wind is blowing; snowflakes float.
I put on my cap and pull it low.
Mittens, boots—I'm ready to go.

Hey! Let's go play in the snow!
Hey! Let's go play in the snow!
Snow is a-falling deep, deep, deep.
I want to make a snowball to keep!

What to Do?

Get little ones excited about fun winter activities with this catchy tune.

(sung to the tune of "I'm a Little Teapot")

It is wintertime; there's lots to do.
We can make snowpals—snow angels too.
We can sled down hills.
We'll slip and slide
Or make igloos to hide inside.

Celebrating Winter

Arts and Crafts

Fluffy Snowpals

Little ones will delight in having these snowy friends hanging around the classroom. In the center of the sticky side of a piece of clear Con-Tact covering, a student makes a snowpal shape with cotton batting. Then she glues on construction paper details, such as a face, a hat, a scarf, and arms. Next, help her smooth another piece of Con-Tact covering over the snowpal and seal the edges. Finally, help her trim around the edges of the snowpal and add a yarn loop near the top of the project for hanging.

Snow Scenes

To give your classroom a little extra sparkle, display these wintry masterpieces. On a light blue sheet of construction paper, a student draws an outdoor scene. He lightly brushes glue on parts of his drawing. To add a snowy sparkle, he sprinkles iridescent glitter or salt on the wet glue. Then he shakes off the excess glitter or salt and sets his paper aside to dry.

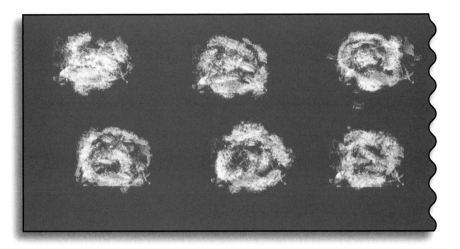

Snowball Painting

Make unique table covers for your winter celebration with this simple idea. To begin, a student wads up a sheet of white paper (snowball). She dips the snowball into white paint and makes several prints on a length of blue bulletin board paper to create a snowy effect.

It's Snowing

Bring winter snow into your classroom with these sparkling snowflakes. On a medium-size paper doily (snowflake), a student squirts dots and lines of glue. Then he sprinkles glitter on the glue and shakes off the excess glitter. When the snowflakes are dry, hang them from the ceiling or display them in a window.

Celebrating Winter

Time to Celebrate!

Matching Mittens

This activity is an art project as well as a matching game. Give each student a pair of identical mitten cutouts (pattern on page 68). A student drips colorful paint on one mitten. Then he places the other mitten on top and smooths his hands over the mittens to spread the paint. He pulls the mittens apart and sets them aside to dry. When the paint is dry, have students sit in a circle. Give each student one of his mittens and place the remaining mittens in the center of the circle. In turn, direct each student to find the match to his mitten and then tape a length of yarn to the mitten pair as shown.

Snowball Relay

Little ones will have a ball participating in this gross-motor game. Invite each child to put on a pair of gloves or mittens and then have students make two lines at one end of an open area. Position a chair or other object opposite each line to designate a turnaround spot for students. Give the first student in each line a small plastic shovel and a white foam ball (snowball). At your signal, the first student in each line balances the snowball on the shovel, walks around the chair and back, and then hands the shovel and snowball to the next student in line. Play continues until each student has had a turn.

Snowpal Favorites

To make a glyph, give each student a snowpal cutout (pattern on page 69). Read aloud the legend below, pausing after each listing so students can follow the directions. Post the completed projects. Then ask glyph-related questions.

Legend

Hat: If you like winter, color the snowpal's hat blue. If you do not like winter, color the snowpal's hat purple.

Face: If you like playing in the snow, draw a happy face on your snowpal. If you do not like playing in the snow, draw a sad face on your snowpal.

Scarf: If you like to go sledding, color the snowpal's scarf green. If you do not like to go sledding, color the snowpal's scarf yellow.

Buttons: If you like hot chocolate, glue three blue pom-poms on your snowpal. If you do not like hot chocolate, glue three red pom-poms on your snowpal.

Arms: If you like soup, glue long brown paper arms to your snowpal. If you do not like soup, glue short brown paper arms to your snowpal.

Frozen Cocoa Pops

Ingredients for one:
⅓ cup water
1 tbsp. hot chocolate mix

Preparation: Personalize a 5 oz. paper cup and gather a craft stick and plastic spoon for each student.

Directions: Instruct each student to put the ingredients in his cup and stir them together. Then place the cups in the freezer. When the mixture begins to solidify, insert a craft stick into each cup. Continue freezing until the pops are solid. Give each child his pop and invite him to tear off the paper cup and enjoy his icy treat.

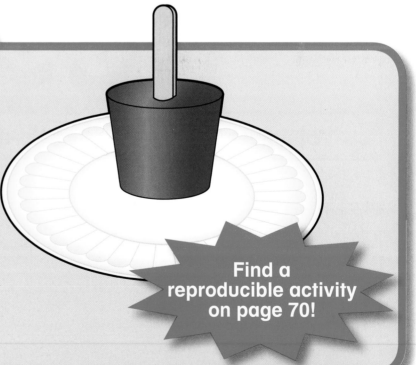

Find a reproducible activity on page 70!

Celebrating Winter

Celebration Planner

To do:

Planned activities:

Reminders:

Volunteer	Contact Number	Email

Hooray for Holidays & Seasonal Celebrations® • ©The Mailbox® Books • TEC61236

We Are Celebrating!

Please join us at _____ on
_____ time
_____, _____,
day   date
as we celebrate _____

_____

_____

_____.

We hope to see you!

A Note for _____

Mitten Pattern
Use with "Matching Mittens" on page 64.

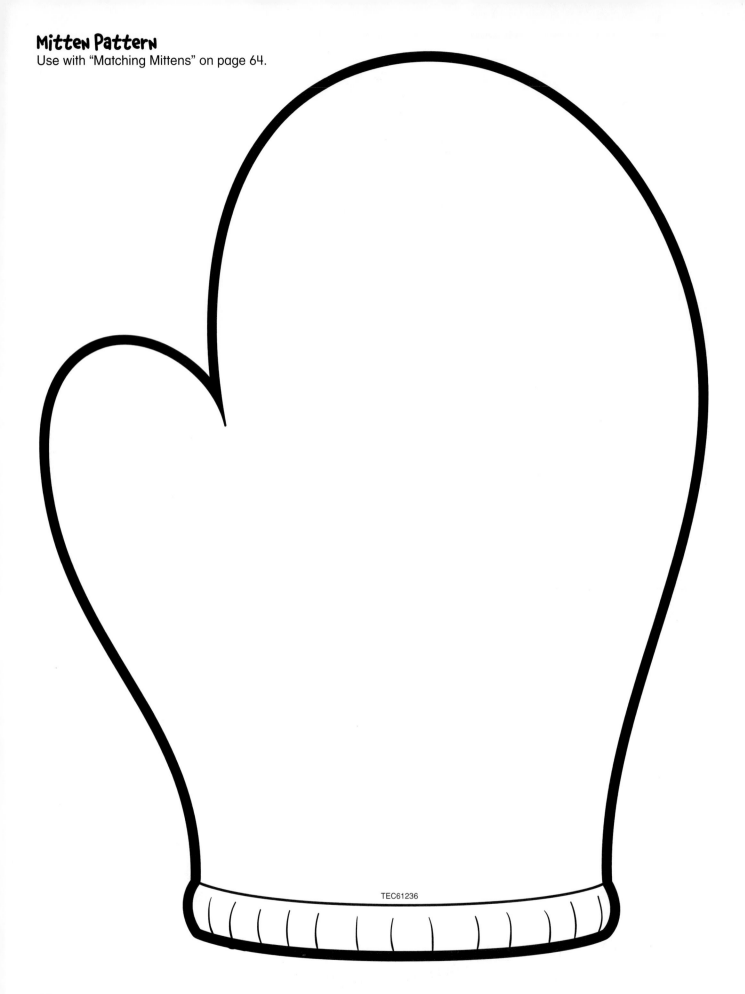

TEC61236

Hooray for Holidays & Seasonal Celebrations® • ©The Mailbox® Books • TEC61236

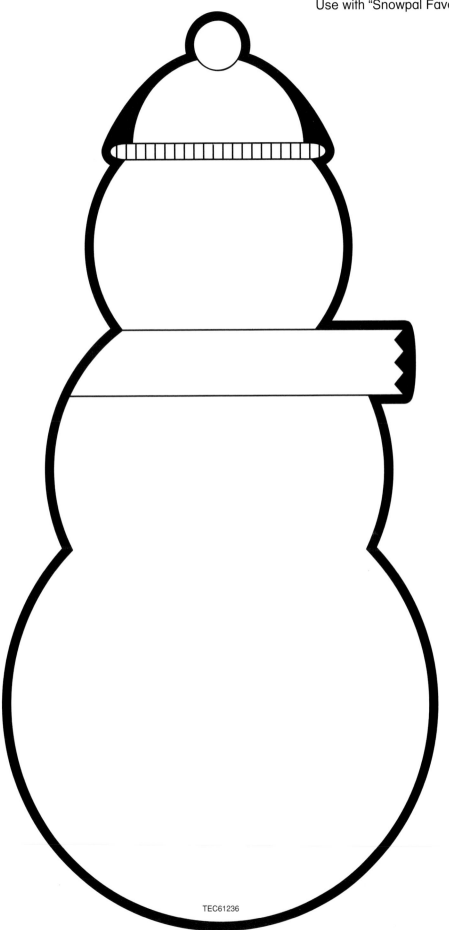

TEC61236

Snowpal Twins

✏️ Color the two snowpals in each row that look the same.

 Hooray for Holidays & Seasonal Celebrations® • ©The Mailbox® Books • TEC61236

Celebrating Valentine's Day

Quick Tips

Calendar Time

- Beginning February 1, attach a heart sticker to your calendar each day until Valentine's Day.
- Attach a character cut from a valentine card to your classroom pointer.

Centers

- Place a variety of valentine cards and envelopes at your writing center for students to sign and address.
- Have students practice one-to-one correspondence by adding large pom-poms to an empty heart-shaped candy box with dividers inside.

Decor

- Have students attach pictures of people and things they love to a large heart cutout labeled "We Love…"

Dismissal

- Blow each student a kiss instead of saying goodbye!

Good Behavior

- Attach class-earned bug stickers to a large heart shape. When a predetermined number of love bugs are on the heart, reward youngsters with a special treat or privilege.

Group Time

- Program the backs of valentine cards with song titles. Choose a card and lead students in singing the corresponding song.
- Attach heart stickers to jumbo craft sticks programmed with students' names. Each day draw a stick and invite that child to wear a heart crown and lead the day's activities.

Delivering Valentines

This sweet song gets little ones thinking about giving valentine cards.

*(sung to the tune of
"The Farmer in the Dell")*

I'll give a valentine
To each good friend of mine.
The cards will say "I love you so!"
And "Be my valentine!"

Plenty of Valentines

In advance, personalize a heart shape for each youngster. After leading students in singing the first verse of the song, show the group a heart and sing that child's name in the second verse. Then present the heart to the child. Repeat the second verse as time allows, choosing a different heart each time.

*(sung to the tune of
"He's Got the Whole World in His Hands")*

I've got valentines in my hands.
I've got valentines in my hands.
I've got valentines in my hands.
I'll give them out for Valentine's Day!

There's one for [Cindy] in my hand.
There's one for [Cindy] in my hand.
There's one for [Cindy] in my hand.
I'll give it out for Valentine's Day!

Celebrating Valentine's Day

A Friendship Wish

Youngsters can sing this song as they distribute Valentine cards or wish their friends a happy Valentine's Day!

(sung to the tune of "My Bonnie Lies Over the Ocean")

I'll send you some valentine wishes
All wrapped up in paper and bows
To tell you our friendship is special
And I'm glad that each day it grows!

Sweet Valentines

Traditional Valentine's Day gifts are the focus of this little ditty.

(sung to the tune of "Twinkle, Twinkle, Little Star")

Will you be my valentine?
I'll be yours, and you'll be mine!
Candy, cards, and flowers too
Can be gifts from me to you.
So let's be sweet valentines.
I'll be yours, and you'll be mine!

Celebrating Valentine's Day

Arts and Crafts

Handy Placemats

These festive placemats are sure to be a favorite of youngsters and parents! To make one, each child lightly dips his hands in a shallow container of paint and makes handprints on a 12" x 18" sheet of paper to form a heart as shown. When the paint is dry, he adds decorations. If desired, laminate the completed placemats for durability.

Antonio

"Heart-y" Centerpieces

This craft looks lovely on a Valentine's Day table at home or in the classroom. To make a valentine centerpiece, a child uses markers or crayons to draw hearts and other valentine-related pictures on both sides of a white paper lunch bag. After he stuffs newspaper strips into the bag, help him gather the middle of the bag and tie it closed with a length of ribbon. Then trim the top of the bag so it looks like a heart.

Celebrating Valentine's Day

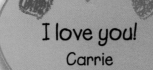

Box of Chocolates

These finished projects look good enough to eat! To make a box of chocolates, a child dips candy-shaped sponges in a shallow container of brown paint and presses them on a large heart shape. Then she drizzles glue tinted with brown paint over each candy print and sets the heart aside to dry. To make a lid, she personalizes a second heart shape and adds a valentine message with your help. After the first heart is dry, staple the hearts together at the top.

Bubbly Heart Art

To prepare, add red paint to a shallow container of bubble solution. A child places a large white heart shape on a newspaper-covered surface. Then she dips a cookie cutter into the bubble mixture, blows the mixture over the paper heart, and watches the bubbles pop onto the paper.

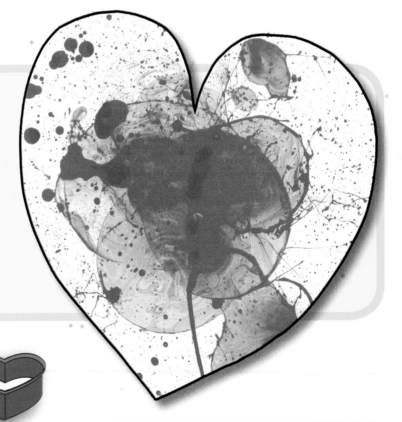

Celebrating Valentine's Day

Time to Celebrate!

Heart Holders

Magnetic note holders make perfect Valentine's Day presents for parents. Have each child draw a self-portrait on a three-inch pink heart cutout. Glue a small bow to the top of the heart; then help each child glue his heart to a wooden clothespin. Attach a strip of magnetic tape to the back of the clothespin to complete the project.

Sweetheart, Sweetheart, Valentine!

Lead little ones in playing this valentine version of the traditional game Duck, Duck, Goose. Seat students in a circle and place a large heart shape in the center. Invite a student volunteer to be It and have her substitute the words *sweetheart* and *valentine* for *duck* and *goose.* If the child who is It is tagged before reaching the valentine's seat, she sits on the heart. The valentine is the next child to be It.

Use your thumbs to make a heart
So I'll remember you when we're apart!

Abby

Emily

Danny

Kyle

Riley

Taryn

Britten

Micah

Mia

Stefan

Alex
name

February 10, 2009
date

Hands-On Valentines

Students are sure to give this memorable keepsake a thumbs-up! Help each child personalize a copy of page 83 and add the date. Then help each child make two thumbprints, as shown, on each classmate's paper and sign her name nearby. When the thumbprints on her paper are dry, she takes it home as a Valentine's Day memento.

Heart Hunt

This game has youngsters searching for hidden hearts. Secretly hide a class supply of small heart shapes around your classroom. Then invite students to hunt for hearts. When a youngster finds a heart, he hands it to you and then assists a classmate in finding one. After each child has located a heart, hide the hearts again for another round of play.

Celebrating Valentine's Day

Love Bugs

Ingredients for one:
mini muffin
frosting
2 small knot-shaped pretzels (wings)
2 mini chocolate chips (eyes)
mini candy-coated chocolate pieces (spots)

Directions: Have each youngster spread frosting on a muffin. Then have her gently press the eyes, wings, and spots in place.

Who's a Sweetheart?

Have students sit in a circle. Quietly play music while students pass a large heart shape around the circle. When the music stops, lead the class in saying, "[Child's name] is a sweetheart!" to the youngster holding the heart. Play continues until each child has been named a sweetheart.

Find a reproducible activity on page 84!

Celebrating Valentine's Day

Celebration Planner

To do:

Planned activities:

Reminders:

Volunteer	Contact Number	Email

It's a Celebration!

Please join us at _____ on
                          time

_____, _____, as we
      day   date

celebrate _____

_____

_____.

We hope to see you!

Hooray for Holidays & Seasonal Celebrations® • ©The Mailbox® Books • TEC61236

Date _____

♡♡ A Heartfelt Note for ♡♡

_____

Hooray for Holidays & Seasonal Celebrations® • ©The Mailbox® Books • TEC61236

Help Us Celebrate Valentine's Day!

Please provide the following for our Valentine's

Day celebration at _____ on

_____ , _____ :

on

time

day   date

_____

_____

_____

Thanks for your help!

Hooray for Holidays & Seasonal Celebrations® • ©The Mailbox® Books • TEC61236

Help Us Celebrate Valentine's Day!

Please provide the following for our Valentine's

Day celebration at _____ on

_____ , _____ :

time

day   date

_____

_____

_____

Thanks for your help!

Hooray for Holidays & Seasonal Celebrations® • ©The Mailbox® Books • TEC61236

Class List

Boys

Girls

Hooray for Holidays & Seasonal Celebrations® • ©The Mailbox® Books • TEC61236

Use your thumbs to make a heart
So I'll remember you when we're apart!

_____   _____
            name   date

Beautiful Balloons

Trace.

Hooray for Holidays & Seasonal Celebrations® • ©The Mailbox® Books • TEC61236

Celebrating St. Patrick's Day

Quick Tips

Centers

- Hide shamrock cutouts in a container of colorful paper shreds and invite students to find them.
- Place at a center green play dough mixed with gold glitter, plastic knives, and a variety of shamrock cookie cutters.

Cleanup

- Play lively Irish music during cleanup time.

Decor

- Have students sponge-paint a large rainbow cutout. Display the finished product with a large pot-of-gold cutout.
- Display around a rainbow students' paintings of leprechauns.

Arrival

- Say, "Top o' the mornin' to ya!" instead of "Good morning!"

Good Behavior

- Reward exceptionally good class behavior by depositing a gold coin cutout in a small jar.

Group Time

- Invite each child to tell about a time he had good luck.

Songs and More

A Shy Leprechaun

Invite your little leprechauns to wave colorful streamers as they sing this song.

(sung to the tune of "If You're Happy and You Know It")

A leprechaun just went outside to play.
He was happy that it was St. Patrick's Day!
He saw rainbows in the sky,
With their colors way up high.
Then he saw me, and he ran the other way.

Are You Wearing Green?

When singing this song, repeat the second verse several times, substituting the names of children who are wearing green.

(sung to the tune of "Row, Row, Row Your Boat")

Are you wearing green?
It's St. Patrick's Day!
If you're wearing something green,
Give a shout—hooray!

[John] is wearing green
On St. Patrick's Day.
[John] is wearing something green.
Give a shout—hooray!

Celebrating St. Patrick's Day

Arts and Crafts

Under the Rainbow

Make these festive headbands in advance so that every child will have something green to wear on St. Patrick's Day. To make one, a child colors a rainbow cutout (pattern on page 92) and glues it to the center of a green paper strip. Then she glues yellow paper circles (gold coins) around her headband as desired. When the glue is dry, staple the paper strip to fit the child's head.

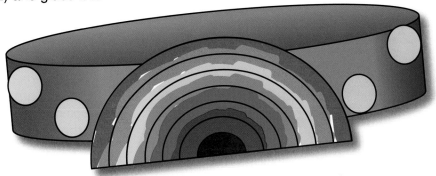

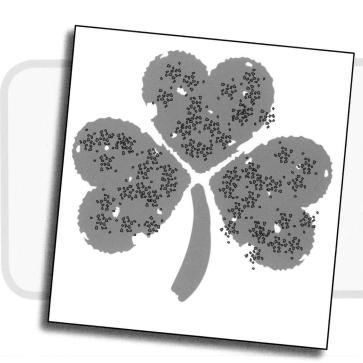

Sparkly Shamrocks

To make a shamrock, a child dips a heart-shaped sponge in a shallow container of green paint and makes a print on the paper. She repeats this process two more times, positioning the prints as shown. Then she paints a stem on the resulting shamrock and sprinkles glitter on the wet paint.

Time to Celebrate!

A Lucky Coin

For this whole-group game, have each student stand in a circle with her hands cupped together in front of her. Choose one child to be the leprechaun and give him a gold coin cutout to hide between his hands. The leprechaun moves around the inside of the circle, putting his hands over the hands of each child. As he moves around the circle, he secretly drops the coin into a classmate's cupped hands. Once the leprechaun has visited every child, he says, "Lucky coin, lucky coin. Who has the lucky coin?" Youngsters take turns guessing who is holding the lucky coin. When the student holding the coin is identified, he becomes the leprechaun for the next round of play.

Rainbow Windsock

These colorful windsocks make festive St. Patrick's Day decorations for the home or classroom. To make one, a child colors half a paper plate so it looks like a rainbow. Then he glues green crepe paper streamers to the bottom edge of the plate half. When the glue is dry, he tapes a green shamrock cutout to the bottom of each streamer. Attach a yarn loop to the top of the plate for a hanger.

Celebrating St. Patrick's Day

Little hat, little tie. 3

A Little Leprechaun

The focus of this kid-size booklet is a tiny leprechaun. For each child, make a copy of the booklet cover and pages on page 92. Read aloud the text on the cover and help each child write her name. Next, read aloud the text on page 1 and have each child color the corresponding clothing green. Continue in this manner with the remaining pages. Then help each child cut apart her pages, stack them in order, and staple the resulting booklet along the side.

Leprechaun Punch

Ingredients for one:
2 frozen cubes of orange-pineapple juice
½ c. lemon-lime Kool-Aid soft drink mix,
    prepared as directed
½ c. lemon-lime soda

Preparation: Have each child color a rainbow cutout (pattern on page 92). Tape her cutout to a disposable cup. Gather a spoon for each child.

Directions: Have each child place the frozen juice cubes in her cup. Then help her pour the lemon-lime drinks into her cup. Have her carefully stir the mixture before taking a drink.

Celebrating St. Patrick's Day

Celebration Planner

To do:

Planned activities:

Reminders:

Volunteer	Contact Number	Email

Hooray for Holidays & Seasonal Celebrations® • ©The Mailbox® Books • TEC61236

Join Our Celebration!

Please join us at _____ on
time

_____, _____,
day   date

as we celebrate _____

_____

_____

_____.

We hope you'll join us!

Hooray for Holidays & Seasonal Celebrations® • ©The Mailbox® Books • TEC61236

A Rainbow of Good News!

Date _____

Hooray for Holidays & Seasonal Celebrations® • ©The Mailbox® Books • TEC61236

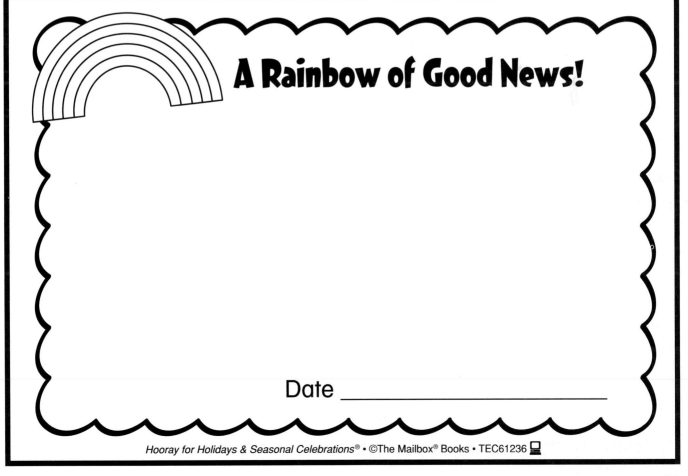

Rainbow Pattern

Use with "Under the Rainbow" on page 87 and "Leprechaun Punch" on page 89.

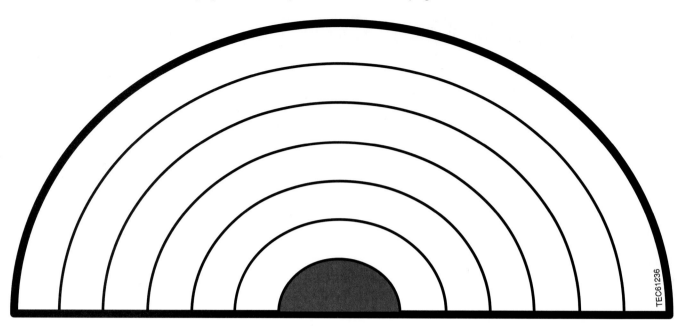

TEC61236

Booklet Cover and Pages

Use with "A Little Leprechaun" on page 89.

A Little Leprechaun

by _____

Hooray for Holidays & Seasonal Celebrations® • ©The Mailbox® Books • TEC61236

Little shirt, little pants.   1

Little jacket, little shoes.   2

Little hat, little tie.   3

Celebrating Spring

Quick Tips

Calendar Time
- Each day, post a cloud, a sun, or a raindrop cutout to chart the weather.

Centers
- Have students sort plastic eggs by color into nests of shredded paper.
- Place a variety of plastic flowers near your sand table and invite students to "plant" a flower garden.

Cleanup
- Encourage students to quietly hop like bunnies during cleanup.

Decor
- Hang blue crepe paper streamers in the room to signify spring's rainy days.
- Decorate the walls with large colorful paper flowers.

Group Time
- Each day, share a nonfiction book about baby animals, birds, or weather.

Rest Time
- Play a recording of birds singing or rain falling as students rest.

Transitions
- Have students pretend to be growing flowers as they stand.

Songs and More

It's Almost Spring

Celebrate the coming of spring by singing this lively tune.

(sung to the tune of "She'll Be Comin' Round the Mountain")

Spring is just around the corner, yes it is.
Spring is just around the corner, yes it is.
[Soon the flowers will be bloomin' and the bees, they will be zoomin'.]
Spring is just around the corner, yes it is.

Additional verses:
Soon the bunnies will be hoppin' and the birds, they will be boppin'.
Soon the rain will fall and fall and the grass, it will grow tall.

Spring Fling

Sing this song to review some of the wonderful things that happen in the spring.

(sung to the tune of "Twinkle, Twinkle, Little Star")

I feel springtime in the air.
Flowers pop up everywhere.
Seeds are planted in a row.
Then we watch our garden grow.
Birds are singing in the trees,
Swaying in the springtime breeze.

Celebrating Spring

Farm Babies

This adorable little ditty helps youngsters remember the names of baby animals.

(sung to the tune of "Sing a Song of Sixpence")

Baby ducks are ducklings,
Yellow powder puffs.
Baby cats are kittens,
Furry balls of fluff.
Baby pigs are piglets.
They love their muddy bath.
Baby geese are goslings,
Honking along their path.

Pretty Tulips

The addition of simple costumes turns this song into an adorable performance. Cut a face-size hole in a class supply of tulip cutouts. As the students sing the song, have them hold the tulips in front of their faces and peek through the holes.

(sung to the tune of "I'm a Little Teapot")

We are pretty tulips, tall and sweet.	*Stand tall.*
Warming in the sun Is such a treat.	*Look up.*
When the breeze is blowing, watch us sway	*Sway from side to side.*
As we brighten up your day.	*Smile.*

Celebrating Spring

Arts and Crafts

Creepy-Crawly Headbands

These headbands are the perfect accessory to wear at a spring celebration. To make a headband, a child accordion-folds six 1" x 8" paper strips (legs) and then glues them to the sides of a tagboard strip (headband). She uses paper scraps and craft materials to add desired details to the headband such as eyes, stripes, spots, or wings.

Designer Flowers

During this activity your little ones create and name a new kind of flower. Display a variety of flower seed packets and discuss the different types of flowers and their names. Then have each student decorate the flower on a copy of page 102. Help him write his name and the name of his flower creation on his seed packet. Next, have him tape a craft stick to the back of the seed packet. Display the completed packets on a piece of bulletin board paper decorated to look like a garden.

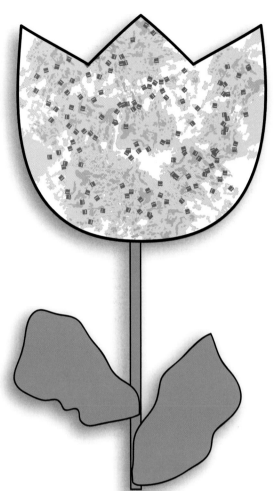

Tall Tulips

These beautiful spring blooms will look great on display in your classroom. A child sponge-paints a large tulip cutout (enlarge the pattern on page 102) and then sprinkles glitter on the wet paint. After the paint is dry, she glues a long green paper strip (stem) to the back of the tulip. Finally, she glues torn green paper leaves on the stem.

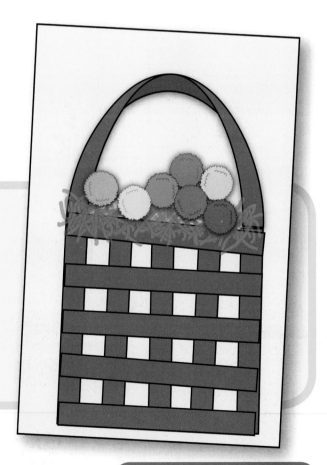

Spring Baskets

Display these baskets to add to the springtime decor of your classroom. To make a basket, a child glues 1" x 9" brown paper strips on a 12" x 18" sheet of construction paper as shown. Then he attaches a 1" x 18" brown paper handle. Next, he brushes glue near the top of the basket and presses cellophane grass into the glue. For the finishing touch, he glues several colorful pom-poms (eggs) on top of the grass.

Celebrating Spring

Time to Celebrate!

Egg Relay

This activity has little ones putting eggs in a nest, just as birds do. Place brown paper shreds in two medium-size tubs to make nests. Arrange the students in two lines in an open area and set a nest opposite each line. Give each student a plastic egg. Hand the first student in each line a spoon and instruct him to put his egg on the spoon. At your signal, have the students with spoons balance their eggs on the spoons as they walk to the nests. When each little one arrives at his line's nest, direct him to drop the egg in the nest, walk back to his line, and give the spoon to the next child in line. Play continues until all the eggs are in the nests.

Rain falls. 3

All About Spring

Your blooming readers will enjoy taking this booklet home and reading it with their families. To make a booklet for each student, staple a cover like the one shown to a set of booklet pages copied and cut out from pages 103–104. Provide crayons and ink pads. Read the text on each page aloud as you help students follow the directions below.

Booklet cover: Write your name.
Booklet page 1: Make a few fingerprints and add details so they look like bugs.
Booklet page 2: Make a few fingerprints and add details so they look like flowers.
Booklet page 3: Make a few blue fingerprints and add details so they look like raindrops.
Booklet page 4: Draw some green grass.
Booklet page 5: Make a few fingerprints and add details so they look like birds.
Booklet page 6: Draw your favorite thing about spring.

Celebrating Spring

What Flowers Need

Plant some springtime fun with this simple idea. Cut the tops off a class supply of clean milk cartons. Each student covers a carton with colorful paper scraps and attaches a copy of a carton label from page 104. Then he scoops potting soil into the bottom half of his carton and puts three marigold seeds on top. He sprinkles more soil on top of the seeds and pats it down. Next, he waters the soil and places the carton on a sunny windowsill. After the seeds sprout, invite students to take their plants home and continue to meet the plants' needs to help them grow.

In this carton I planted seeds.
Please help me meet
Their simple needs:
Water and sunlight
To help them grow.
Then we'll have flowers
With a sunny glow!

Eggs in a Nest

Ingredients for one:
plastic knife
rice cake
prepared butterscotch pudding
chow mein noodles
round cereal pieces (eggs)

Directions: Instruct each child to spread some pudding on her rice cake with a plastic knife. Then have her place noodles on the pudding to make a nest. Finally, direct her to put a few eggs in the nest.

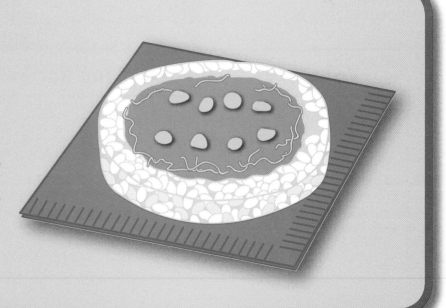

Celebrating Spring

Celebration Planner

To do:

Planned activities:

Reminders:

Volunteer	Contact Number	Email

Hooray for Holidays & Seasonal Celebrations® • ©The Mailbox® Books • TEC61236

We Are Celebrating!

Please join us at _____ on

time

_____, _____,

day　　　　　　　　　date

as we celebrate _____

_____

_____

_____.

We hope to see you!

Hooray for Holidays & Seasonal Celebrations® • ©The Mailbox® Books • TEC61236

A Note for _____

Hooray for Holidays & Seasonal Celebrations® • ©The Mailbox® Books • TEC61236

Seed Packet Pattern

Use with "Designer Flowers" on page 96.

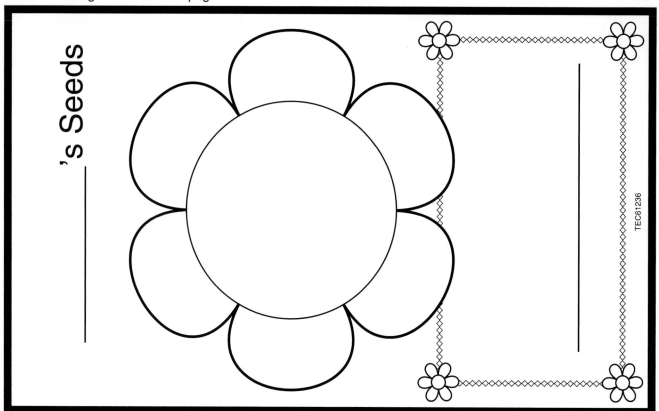

Tulip Pattern

Use with "Tall Tulips" on page 97.

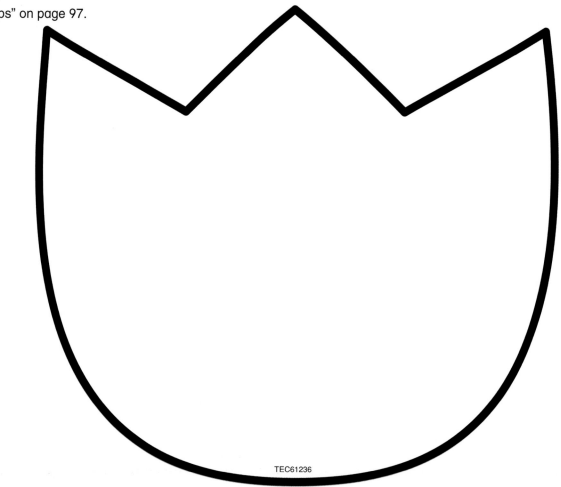

TEC61236

Bugs zoom!

1

Flowers bloom.

2

Rain falls.

3

Grass grows tall.

4

Booklet Pages

Use with "All About Spring" on page 98.

Birds sing.

5

I love spring!

6

Hooray for Holidays & Seasonal Celebrations® • ©The Mailbox® Books • TEC61236

Carton Labels

Use with "What Flowers Need" on page 99.

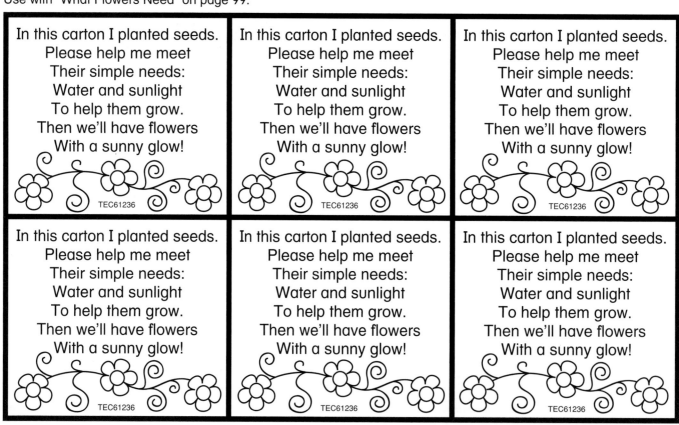

In this carton I planted seeds.
Please help me meet
Their simple needs:
Water and sunlight
To help them grow.
Then we'll have flowers
With a sunny glow!
TEC61236

In this carton I planted seeds.
Please help me meet
Their simple needs:
Water and sunlight
To help them grow.
Then we'll have flowers
With a sunny glow!
TEC61236

In this carton I planted seeds.
Please help me meet
Their simple needs:
Water and sunlight
To help them grow.
Then we'll have flowers
With a sunny glow!
TEC61236

In this carton I planted seeds.
Please help me meet
Their simple needs:
Water and sunlight
To help them grow.
Then we'll have flowers
With a sunny glow!
TEC61236

In this carton I planted seeds.
Please help me meet
Their simple needs:
Water and sunlight
To help them grow.
Then we'll have flowers
With a sunny glow!
TEC61236

In this carton I planted seeds.
Please help me meet
Their simple needs:
Water and sunlight
To help them grow.
Then we'll have flowers
With a sunny glow!
TEC61236

Celebrating Parents

Quick Tips

Calendar Time

- In May, mark Mother's Day with a flower cutout, and in June mark Father's Day with a necktie cutout. Each month, count the days until the designated holiday.

Centers

- At your writing center, place decorative paper and envelopes. Encourage youngsters to write letters to their moms, their dads, or other special adults.
- Set out a variety of craft supplies at your art center and invite students to make a portrait of one of their parents.

Good Behavior

- Each time your students exhibit exceptionally good behavior, attach a foil-wrapped candy kiss–shaped cutout to a display. Reward students with a special treat or privilege when they've collected a predetermined number of kisses and send a note home to their parents to let them know the good news.

Group Time

- Invite each little one to share with the group a photo of her mom or dad and tell about her or him.
- Invite parents to read aloud to the class.

Transitions

- Announce a hair color and invite students who have a parent with the corresponding hair color to line up.
- When you have a few extra moments, invite youngsters to name ways they can show their parents they appreciate them.

Songs and More

My Mommy

Invite each youngster to proclaim his love for his mom with this heartfelt tribute.

(sung to the tune of "Clementine")

I love Mommy!
I love Mommy!
She does oh-so-much for me!
How I love her, none above her,
The best mom you'll ever see!

The Best Daddy

Lead little ones in adding hand motions to make this sweet tune a delightful performance!

(sung to the tune of "He's Got the Whole World in His Hands")

I've got the best daddy in the world!
I've got the best daddy in the world!
I've got the best daddy in the world!
So I say, "Happy Father's Day!"

Celebrating Parents

Arts and Crafts

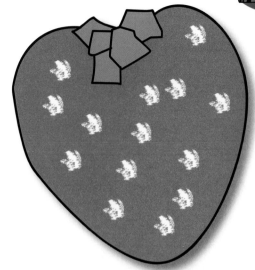

A "Berry" Fine Card

In honor of Mother's Day, have little ones make these sweet cards for their moms or other special ladies. For each child, cut a heart-shaped card from a 12" x 18" sheet of red construction paper and round the point to make the heart resemble a strawberry. A youngster glues green paper scraps to the top of her strawberry card to make a stem. Then she dips her pinkie finger into white paint and presses it on the strawberry to make seeds. When the paint is dry, help her write a message inside the card similar to the one shown.

You are the "berry" best Mom!

Love, Carly

Super Dad!

Super Dad!

These magnetic clips make great Father's Day gifts! Have each little one color a copy of a badge pattern from page 112. Next, help him cut out the badge and glue it to a wooden clothespin. Then attach a strip of magnetic tape to the back of the clothespin to complete the project.

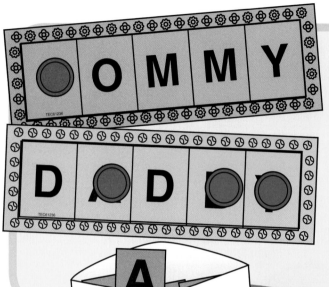

Parent Matchup

To prepare for this partner game, make two copies of the gameboards on page 112. Cut apart one pair of gameboards, mix up the resulting cards, and then place them in an envelope. Cut the remaining gameboards as shown; then give one gameboard to each child. To play, a child chooses a card from the envelope. If it matches a letter on her gameboard, she covers the corresponding letter with a marker and sets the card aside. If it does not match a letter on her gameboard, she returns the card to the envelope. The pair takes turns until one player has covered each letter on her gameboard.

Mom or Dad?

Ingredients for one:

rice cake
cream cheese tinted various skin tones
sliced fruits and vegetables
shredded coconut tinted various hair
    colors

Directions: Have each child spread tinted cream cheese on a rice cake. Then have him use the fruits, vegetables, and coconut to make a snack that resembles his mom or dad.

Celebrating Parents

It's a Match!

Have each youngster bring in a photo of herself with her mom or dad (or another special adult). If a child is unable to bring in a photo, have someone take a photo of her with you. Puzzle-cut each photo in half. Attach half of each photo to a sheet of bulletin board paper and place the remaining halves in an envelope. A child takes a photo half from the envelope and matches it to the corresponding photo half on the paper. She continues until she has correctly matched each photo.

Handmade Certificates

Invite little ones to make certificates proclaiming that their moms or dads are the best! Make a blank certificate similar to the one shown and copy it to make a class supply. Help each child label the certificate with his chosen person's name and title; then help him sign and date it. Provide a variety of stamps, stickers, adhesive seals and craft supplies and have each child decorate his certificate as desired.

This certifies that

Kathryn Montana
name

is the best   Mom

in the world.

Owen   5-12-10
signed   date

Celebration Planner

To do:

Planned activities:

Reminders:

Volunteer	Contact Number	Email

Hooray for Holidays & Seasonal Celebrations® • ©The Mailbox® Books • TEC61236

Come Join Us!

We are celebrating _____

on _____ , _____ ,
          day   date

at _____ . It will
        time

be a lot of fun!

We hope to see you!

Thank You, Parents!

Badge Patterns
Use with "Super Dad!" on page 107.

Gameboard Patterns
Use with "Parent Matchup" on page 108.

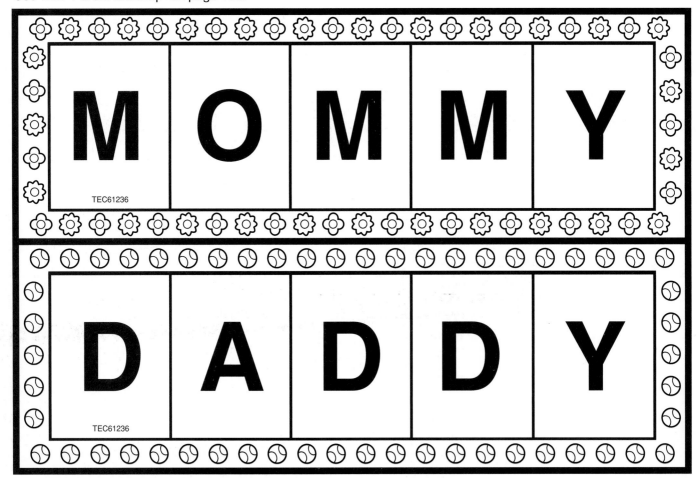

Celebrating Graduation

Quick Tips

Calendar Time

- Use a rolled piece of paper tied with a ribbon (diploma) as your classroom pointer.
- Mark Graduation Day on your calendar. Each day, count the days until graduation.

Centers

- Put students' favorite toys, props, and manipulatives from the year at a center.
- Place paper, markers, and school-themed stickers in your writing center and have students create their own diplomas.

Cleanup

- Play a recording of "Pomp and Circumstance" to signal cleanup time.

Dismissal

- Substitute "Good luck, graduates!" for "Goodbye!"

Group Time

- Invite students to sing or perform their favorite songs or fingerplays from the year.

Songs and More

A Great Year!

Singing this song reminds youngsters of the past school year.

(sung to the tune of "Do Your Ears Hang Low?")

School is almost done,
And we have had so much fun.
We have made lots of good friends,
And we really like each one.
Now we'll have a lot of free time
Because summertime is here.
School is almost done.

It's Graduation Time

This sweet song is a great way for little ones to thank parents, volunteers, and school staff who helped during the school year.

(sung to the tune of "My Bonnie Lies Over the Ocean")

It is time for our graduation.
It's time for us to say goodbye.
It is time for our graduation.
Oh my, how the time does fly!

Thank you, thank you,
Thank you for all of your help this year.
Thank you, thank you,
Thank you for all of your help.

Arts and Crafts

Memory Tablecloths

Invite little ones to take a stroll down memory lane while making table coverings for your graduation celebration. Encourage each student to tell his favorite memory from the school year, such as a special event, field trip, or visitor. Then on several lengths of bulletin board paper write "Memories." Have each student draw his favorite memory on one of the papers and dictate a sentence about his drawing.

The firefighter's truck had lots of cool stuff on it.

Erin
is graduating!

Picture Perfect

These pleasing portraits will remind students of their graduation day for years to come. Help each student personalize a copy of page 120. A child colors the face so it resembles her own and colors her cap and gown as desired. She glues yarn pieces to the portrait so they look like her hair. Then she traces the tassel with glue, sprinkles glitter on the glue, and shakes off the excess glitter.

Celebrating Graduation

Friendship Posters

Help youngsters remember their classmates with these fun-to-make keepsakes. Make a class supply of posters from light blue poster board and write "A Cool School!" on the front of each. Write each student's name on the back of his poster. On each of his classmates' posters, as well as his own, a child sponge-paints a fish and writes his name by the fish. When his poster is dry, the child uses a black marker to add eyes and a mouth to the fish on his poster.

Remember When?

Review events from the school year with this fun game. Prior to playing the game, have each child program both sides of a blank card as shown. To play, ask about a real or fictitious school event, beginning your question with "Remember when…" Then ask each youngster to hold up his card with the correct answer facing out. Next, invite student volunteers to take turns asking questions about class events. Continue until each child has had a turn.

Graduation Cap

Ingredients for one:
paper plate
unwrapped caramel cup candy
  piece
chocolate graham cracker square
chocolate frosting
piece of thin licorice (tassel)

Directions:
　　To make a cap, have a student place the caramel cup upside down on a plate and use frosting to attach the graham cracker to the cup. Then direct her to put another dab of frosting on top of the graham cracker and press one end of the tassel in the frosting.

Graduation Diploma

Ingredients for one:
slice of bread with crust removed
jam
piece of thin licorice (ribbon)

Directions: To make a diploma, have a student spread jam on the bread slice and roll it up as shown. Then have him tie the licorice ribbon around the diploma.

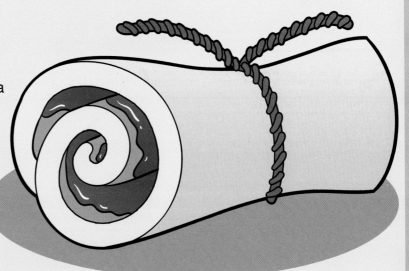

Celebrating Graduation

Celebration Planner

To do:

Planned activities:

Reminders:

Volunteer	Contact Number	Email

Hooray for Holidays & Seasonal Celebrations • ©The Mailbox® Books • TEC61236

We Are Celebrating!

Please join us at _____ on
                        time

_____, _____,
       day   date

                                as we celebrate

_____

_____

_____

_____.

We hope to see you!

Hooray for Holidays & Seasonal Celebrations® • ©The Mailbox® Books • TEC61236

_____
                name

Have a Great Summer!

From _____

Hooray for Holidays & Seasonal Celebrations® • ©The Mailbox® Books • TEC61236

is graduating!

Hooray for Holidays & Seasonal Celebrations® • ©The Mailbox® Books • TEC61236

120   **Note to the teacher:** Use with "Picture Perfect" on page 115.

Celebrating Summer

Quick Tips

Centers

- Float Ping-Pong balls (beach balls), plastic boats, and toy dolls in your water table.
- Bury large seashells in a container of sand and have students find them.

Cleanup

- Provide plastic sand buckets and shovels for students to use during cleanup.
- Invite little ones to wear sunglasses as they search for trash to pick up off the floor.

Decor

- Place an empty wading pool in your reading corner.

Good Behavior

- When the class has exceptionally good behavior, attach a paper strip (ray) to a large circle cutout (sun).

Group Time

- Place a few pictures of summertime foods in the bottom row of a pocket chart. Then help students use name cards to make a graph displaying their food preferences.
- Pass a beach ball to a youngster to indicate her turn to talk.

Rest Time

- Play a recording of soothing ocean waves as students rest.

Songs and More

The Shining Sun

Incorporate summer props to turn this sunny song into a musical production!

(sung to the tune of "If You're Happy and You Know It")

When the summer sun shines brightly, wear sunscreen.
When the summer sun shines brightly, wear sunscreen.
When the summer sun shines brightly, a sunburn is very likely.
When the summer sun shines brightly, wear sunscreen.

When the summer sun shines brightly, wear a hat.
When the summer sun shines brightly, wear a hat.
When the summer sun shines brightly, find a hat to pull on tightly.
When the summer sun shines brightly, wear a hat.

When the summer sun shines brightly, find some shade.
When the summer sun shines brightly, find some shade.
When the summer sun shines brightly, find some shade and cool off slightly.
When the summer sun shines brightly, find some shade.

Feeling Hot!

Youngsters and parents alike won't be able to resist singing and performing this cool little ditty.

(sung to the tune of "The Itsy-Bitsy Spider")

When it's really hot outside	*Draw hand across brow.*
And I want to keep cool,	*Fan face with hand.*
I squirt the hose	*Pretend to squirt a hose.*
Or dive into the pool.	*Pantomime a dive.*
I like the lake	*Smile and nod.*
For swimming when it's hot,	*Pretend to swim.*
But splashing in the ocean	*Pantomime jumping a wave.*
Is what I like a lot!	*Point to self and nod.*

Celebrating Summer

Arts and Crafts

Sandy Placemats

Surf into summer with these beach-themed placemats. To make one, a child decorates a 12" x 18" sheet of light blue construction paper with seashell cutouts, beach-themed stickers, and drawings. Then she brushes glue on desired areas of the placemat and sprinkles craft sand on the glue. Finally, she shakes off the excess sand. Laminate the completed placemats for durability.

Sunflower Centerpieces

These tall table toppers showcase a sunny sign of summer! To make a sunflower, a child paints a cardboard tube green (stem) and the outside of two small paper plates yellow (petals). After the paint dries, help him sandwich the tube between the plates as shown; then staple the plate rims together. To complete his sunflower, he glues small black pom-poms (seeds) to the center of one plate. Display the flowers by securing the base of each stem in a ball of clay and placing them on tables and desks as desired.

Time to Celebrate!

A Perfectly Packed Picnic

To prepare for this whole-group game, place in a covered basket several picnic items, such as a paper plate, a plastic spoon, a napkin, and an assortment of plastic food. Show the basket to the group; then give clues about the items inside. For example, to describe the plate you might say, "The object is round and white. You put food on it. It is made from paper." When a student correctly names an item, remove it from the basket and display it in front of the group. Continue until each item in the basket has been revealed.

I like to swim in my Grandma's swimming pool.

Fun in the Sun

Invite youngsters to make posters illustrating their favorite sunny weather activities. Have each child glue a six-inch yellow circle (sun) to the top half of a vertically positioned 12" x 18" sheet of construction paper. Ask her to draw rays around the cutout. Then have her draw and color on the bottom half of the paper a picture of herself engaged in her favorite summer activity. When she's finished, help her write on a blank card a caption that describes her drawing and attach it to her paper.

A Seashell Salad

Ingredients for one:
cooked shell pasta (served cold)
shredded mozzarella cheese
ranch dressing

Preparation: Have each child color an ocean wave cutout. Tape her cutout to a disposable bowl.

Directions: Have each child scoop a ladleful of pasta into her bowl and sprinkle some cheese on top. Help her squirt ranch dressing on the pasta and then stir her salad. Finally, invite her to dive in and taste the scrumptious snack she's made!

Barefoot in the grass.
1

The Barefoot Booklet

Your little ones will be head over heels for this booklet activity! In advance, make a white construction paper copy of page 128 for each child. Read aloud the text on the cover and help each child write her name. Next, read aloud the text on page 1 and have each child draw an illustration of herself to match the text. Continue with the remaining pages. Then help each child cut out her pages, stack them in order atop the backing, and staple the resulting booklet at the top.

Celebrating Summer

Celebration Planner

To do:

Planned activities:

Reminders:

Volunteer	Contact Number	Email

Hooray for Holidays & Seasonal Celebrations® • ©The Mailbox® Books • TEC61236

Celebrate
Summer With Us!

Please join us at _____ on
time

_____, _____,
day _date_

as we celebrate _____

_____.

We hope to see you!

Hooray for Holidays & Seasonal Celebrations® • ©The Mailbox® Books • TEC61236

Date _____

_____
name

has some "sun-sational" news!

Hooray for Holidays & Seasonal Celebrations® • ©The Mailbox® Books • TEC61236

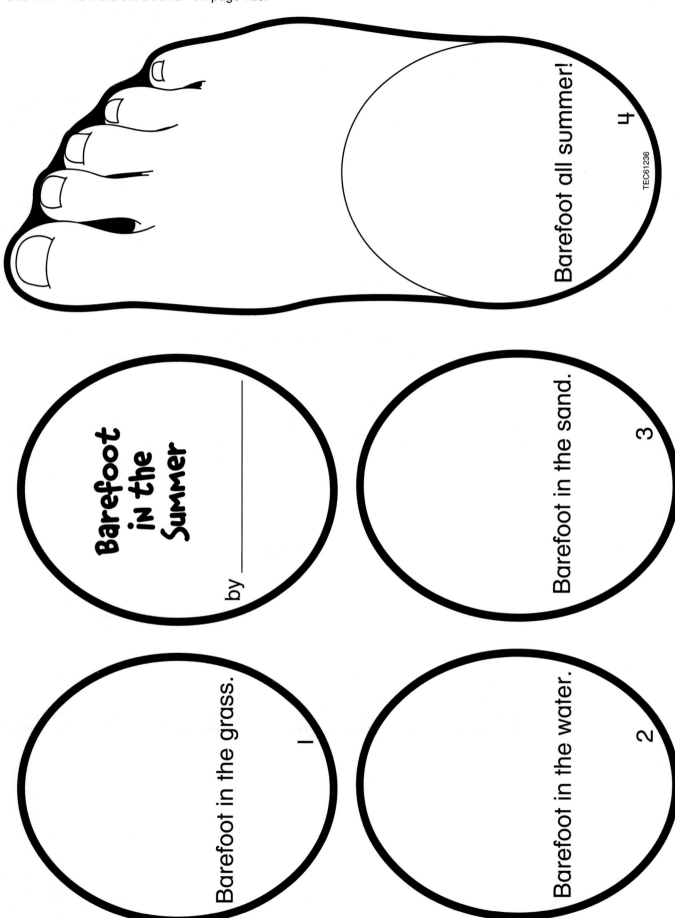

Barefoot all summer!

4

TEC61236

Barefoot in the Summer

by _____

Barefoot in the sand.

3

Barefoot in the grass.

1

Barefoot in the water.

2

Hooray for Holidays & Seasonal Celebrations® • ©The Mailbox® Books • TEC61236